THE
FOUR
ELEMENTS
OF
SUCCESS

A SIMPLE PERSONALITY PROFILE
THAT WILL TRANSFORM YOUR TEAM

LAURIE BETH JONES

NELSON BUSINESS
A Division of Thomas Nelson Publishers
Since 1798

www.thomasnelson.com

Published in Nashville, Tennessee, by Thomas Nelson, Inc.

Nelson Books titles may be purchased in bulk for educational, business, fundraising, or sales promotional use. For information, please e-mail SpecialMarkets@ThomasNelson.com.

Unless otherwise noted, the Scripture quotations are from THE NEW KING JAMES VERSION. Copyright © 1979, 1980, 1982, Thomas Nelson, Inc., Publishers.

Scripture quotations noted JERUSALEM BIBLE are from THE JERUSALEM BIBLE. Copyright © 1966 by Darton, Longman & Todd Ltd. and Doubleday & Company, Inc. Used by permission.

Library of Congress Cataloging-in-Publication Data

Jones, Laurie Beth.
    The four elements of success : a simple personality profile that will transform your team / Laurie Beth Jones.
        p. cm.
    Includes bibliographical references.
    ISBN: 0-7852-0888-7 (hardcover)
    ISBN: 0-7852-8810-4 (trade paper)
    1. Teams in the workplace—Management. 2. Personality and motivation. 3. Personality assessment. 4. employee selection. 5. Organizational effectiveness. I. Title: Personality profile that will transform your team. II. Title.
    HD66.J6547 2005
    658.4'022—dc22   2005003497

Printed in the United States of America

06 07 08 09 10 RRD 5 4 3 2

To you, my readers,
who make these words come alive.

CONTENTS

III. The 28-Day Challenge

Appendices

PREFACE

In the beginning God created the heavens and the earth. Now the earth was a formless void, there was darkness over the deep, and God's spirit hovered over the water. God said, "Let there be light," and there was light.

—GENESIS 1:1–3 (JERUSALEM BIBLE)

This opening passage in Genesis tells us that all the building blocks of the universe are contained in the elements: the formless earth, the deep waters, the divine wind, and the creation of light, or fire. My prayer is that this book will be a genesis for you as well. May you, too, take the elemental makeup of your own personality, and that of your team, and create something amazing that never existed before.

Laurie Beth Jones

INTRODUCTION

Ashes to ashes. Dust to dust. In the end all of us are reduced to some form of earth. Just as *Adam* means "taken from the clay," each of us is an amazing blend of the earth of calcium and the water of cells, the fire of synapses and the breath of life.

I read that if the human body were reduced to its chemical components, it would be worth about $1.76. But we human beings are worth so much more than that. With fingerprints like snowflakes—no two alike—we are energy-filled, action-oriented phenomena capable of creating symphonies, curing diseases, building universities, and risking our lives on behalf of others.

We are born alone, and we die alone. And yet in the middle of that experience, we have an innate need and desire to form teams, to bond with others in fascinating, frustrating, and fulfilling ways to create something new.

That is the joy and power, beauty and promise, of this thing we call "teams." Whether it is the team of two deciding to get married and raise a family or a team of seventy executives leading a billion-dollar enterprise, the ability to form meaningful and creative bonds is the essence of civilization.

Ultimately all human progress depends on teamwork. What

causes some teams to win and others to lose? What allows a small group of highly committed individuals to outsmart and outmaneuver teams far larger and more financially well endowed? What causes some marriages to succeed and others to fail? What causes some people to go home at night and want to pull out their hair, while others can't wait to get out of bed and head to the workplace?

In this book I will present information and insights on the four basic elements of earth, water, wind, and fire. I will demonstrate how each of us contains all of them, yet one or two elements will particularly dominate and drive our behaviors, attitudes, and actions. I call this program the Path Elements Profile™ (PEP). In the last seven years since I have been testing and teaching it, this program has been used successfully by teachers, therapists, CEOs, youth workers, business and spiritual leaders, stay-at-home moms, and family counselors. Insights surrounding PEP have helped save marriages, unite families, discern career directions, and select everything from jobs to spouses.

Understanding and utilizing this personality profile tool will revolutionize your understanding of who you are and help you clarify why you do the things you do. It will help you focus on your strengths and understand the challenges that have been hindering you, perhaps unnamed, for years. With this information you will be able to anticipate and thus prevent unnecessary tensions and arguments before they start. It will help you understand and recruit team members as well as put together teams of significance and power.

With your new knowledge of the four elements, you will also have keen insights into the needs and values of others and thus be more persuasive when it comes to getting your own needs met. The four elements technology will guide you when making important job or career decisions. It will help you understand your spouse, children, in-laws, boss, coworkers, suppliers, and customers better. And most of all, it is fun and easy to use.

How and Why I
Developed This Concept

After my first book, *Jesus, CEO*, was published and hit *Business Week*'s bestseller list, I received hundreds of invitations from organizations around the country to speak on the topic of leadership. Since leadership means "the ability to influence others to take a certain course of action," I was most interested in creating tools that helped people move themselves and others forward faster.

Having been exposed to the many fine personality profiles on the market today, I still lacked a tool that was simple, visual, intuitive, and powerful enough to create a shift in thinking as well as relating. Thus, I developed what has come to be known as the Path Elements Profile™, or PEP.

Most personality-type assessments today are based on the fourfold personality types. DISC is one example that comes to mind as well as the more ancient type, that of phlegmatic, choleric, sanguine, and I forget the other one. Literally. Which is one of the challenges of word-based personality type assessments. The Myers-Briggs Type Indicator® is excellent if you are an academic and want a detailed and intense profile. I took the Myers-Briggs, yet to this day I can't remember what order my initials were supposed to be in . . . NFSJT? LMNOP? In an informal survey of 100 people who had taken at least four personality assessments, only three could remember accurately what their particular type was. If you can't remember it, how can you apply it? I share this not to denigrate other fine systems, but to show why I, in my desire for simplicity and memorability, sought and invented something else.

The elemental personality assessment was born out of the frustration I felt when asking corporate leaders this question: "Who are you?" The answers were invariably either a job description ("I'm a CPA") or a role ("I'm a husband [or wife]"). These words described not who they were, but what they did as well as what roles they played. They had little or nothing to do with each person's unique essence.

Recognizing the importance of self-image, I decided to use the four elements of earth, water, wind, and fire to help people in their self-identity process.

Jesus referred to Himself as "living water." In the Scriptures the Holy Spirit is described as being "wind" or "fire." *Adam* literally means "made from clay."

Most nonwestern cultures understand and respect the elements. Native Americans used to pray to the elements to bless their crops as well as their battles. The Chinese term *feng shui*, which is the art of optimum placement of inanimate objects to create harmony, actually means "wind and water." Hindus use the elements in their healing rituals and baths. The Kabbalah, a form of Jewish mysticism, reveals that the four symbols representing the Hebrew YHWH, or *Yahweh*, actually are a tetragrammaton that stands for the four elements of earth, water, air, and fire.

Psychologist Carl Jung wrote about the elements, believing that each of us has some measure of them within us. He called it "the Quaternity." His theories of the fourfold personality became the foundation for much of the personality theories in use today.

When I first began introducing my theory regarding personalities and the elements, some of my more conservative Christian friends expressed alarm, believing that this material sounded a bit too New Age. When I reminded them that Jesus called Himself "living water," and that the book of Genesis opens with an overview of the elements, they calmed down a little bit.

Other friends asked if the elements related to their astrological signs. My mother and father were born on the exact same day in the exact same year—January 18, 1920. That would have made both of them the same astrological sign, yet they could not have been more different than night and day. As a Christian, I was taught that we must look to God, rather than the stars, to determine our destiny. For my purposes and the purposes of this book, there is no direct correlation between one's sign, birth date, and the four elements.

People may behave like the descriptions accompanying their astrological signs more as a direct result of the prophetic image that was created in their minds rather than actual correlations. A person born as a Taurus, for example, may identify with the stubbornness of a bull and then begin to claim that image and trait for herself.

Likewise, I am aware that the images of wind or water, earth or fire, may become prophetic for people who take the characteristics of their elements, desired or otherwise, and begin to act them out.

I remain firmly rooted in my Christian faith and tradition, and I believe that the elements are fascinating reflections of the different characteristics of God, the Creator, yet have no separate divine powers in and of themselves. In other words, don't pray to water; pray to the God who created it.

TAKING THE FIRST STEPS WITH PEP

In my Path training seminars, I asked people to write down or call out the positive characteristics of each element, one at a time: "What positive characteristics come to mind when you think of earth?" Slowly people suggested words like *solid, round, fertile,* and *predictable.* By the time we reached the fourth element of fire, people were invariably laughing and calling out words like *hot, mesmerizing, consuming,* and *passionate!* This warm-up exercise quickly became one of the most engaging and popular parts of the seminar.

What I Began to See

Gray-suited CEOs began canceling prior appointments with others in order to stay later and talk with me about what they had learned about themselves through the PEP exercises. When I went on break, I returned to find them copying the information that was on my overhead projector so that they could take it back to their

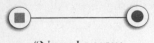

companies. A Fortune 50 company asked to be certified in the training to use with thousands of employees.

As I traveled the country and spoke in venues from convents to Fortune 50 international headquarters, I found that people from all walks of life, from different professions and even religions, could readily and eagerly engage in the dialogue around Earth, Water, Wind, and Fire. As I trained my Path facilitators in these techniques, I received reports of lives changed, marriages healed, conflicts resolved, and businesses moving forward at lightning speed.

For example, after introducing this concept to a group of 250 business leaders, I was surprised when a man stood up and bellowed, "Now I know why I've been frustrated with my company the last fifteen years. I am Fire working in an Earth organization!" He quit that company and started his own.

Another CEO in a different setting stood with eyes wide open as I asked the people who were Earth on his team to gather in one part of the room, people who were Water to cluster over in another part, Wind next to them, and Fire next to me. The room almost tilted as seventy-six of his one-hundred-member team stampeded into the Earth corner. Remaining in the other corners were seventeen Waters, six Winds, and only one Fire, who happened to be the CEO. He looked at the elemental makeup of his team and said, "You just did in fifteen minutes what I have been paying consultants thousands of dollars to try to understand. No wonder I can't get anything to move around here!"

One woman in a seminar stated, "This knowledge could have helped prevent my last two divorces. I am a Wind, always attracted to Earths. Things go fine for a while, but soon they start complaining, saying things like, 'Do we have to go on another trip?' or 'Who is going to feed the cats and collect the mail while we're gone?'"

When we taught PEP as part of a two-day Path for Teens training seminar, one woman reported, "Last night my daughter came in and sat down and said, 'Mom, I get it. You are Wind, and I am Fire. No wonder we get into arguments so easily. The truth is, we really do need each other. We just need to find a way not to put each other out!'" (This from a fourteen-year-old.)

A friend of mine, who is a missionary, took the PEP concept to a training he did in South Africa. He said in amazement, "Laurie Beth, even the children get this! They were so excited about their elements, running around telling their families and friends. It gives them positive images that they can claim immediately for themselves."

PEP works. The elements are fun. Kids get it. Adults talk about it. People who have been through the training begin to use the terms to relate to others: "Oh, there's the Wind in you talking," or "Here comes a blistering memo from Fire again." Invariably after we have done a PEP training in organizations, those who missed the training felt left out because suddenly there was a new vocabulary floating around that they did not understand. Having an exciting and fun and descriptive vocabulary that explains immediately both the challenges and the strengths of diversity is one of the most priceless benefits of this tool.

The book is divided into ten chapters. In Chapter 1 you will gain a renewed understanding and respect for the positive characteristics and the challenges of each element. You will be able to read through the elemental descriptions and quickly choose which one, or two, you most relate to. I will ask you to seek feedback from your friends about the element you are most like, which in itself may prove the worth of this book. Their answers may upset, surprise, or delight you, but they will most definitely inform you about how others see you.

Once you have an understanding of your top one or two elemental tendencies, we will go deeper into the application in Chapter 2.

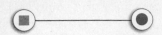

WHILE THE IDEAL
STATE IS THAT
PEOPLE WILL KEEP
THEIR WORK LIVES
AND THEIR HOME
LIVES SEPARATE,
THE TRUTH IS,
THEY DON'T.

Here we will immediately apply your newfound understanding in the areas where most of us live, which is euphemistically called "interpersonal relationships." While the ideal state is that people will keep their work lives and their home lives separate, the truth is, they don't. Therefore, this chapter will present practical case studies and examples to show how using the knowledge of the elements can smooth and soothe the way for you, your spouse, family, friends, and coworkers.

In Chapter 3, you will begin to see how to use this knowledge in the all-important arena of team dynamics. This chapter is for anyone who is working with others to accomplish a goal, which should include just about everybody. It is especially geared toward those who must use their teams to accomplish highly specific and competitive tasks, especially in the business world.

Chapter 4 covers using the Elements to grow (and retain) your team.

Chapter 5 will explore the fun world of how to use your knowledge of the four elements to improve customer understanding as well as increase your personal skills in persuasion.

In Chapter 6, we will explore the elements and their unique blends in relationship to career choices, for you personally and for your team members.

In Chapters 7 through 10, I will reveal twenty-eight of the best practices employed by world-class companies. I have included a quiz and a checklist to enable you to see how your company compares. I have placed the twenty-eight principles into four subcategories of Fire, Earth, Water, and Wind, and provided solid examples of what is working in the real world. I also will challenge you to a twenty-eight-day transformation journey; if you follow these twenty-eight principles, you and your team will be transformed.

The Appendices include additional material that might prove helpful in understanding the concepts, including some commonly asked questions.

There are several strategic advantages in reading and using *The Four Elements of Success*:

1. It is simple. Other tools on the market are complex and heavily analytical.

2. It is intuitive. Almost anyone can relate to the elements.

3. It is fun. Discussions around the elements offer rich metaphors for use in nonjudgmental team building.

4. It can be put to use immediately in multiple settings.

5. It is sticky. Once you know your element(s), you will never forget them.

When I look back on my personal life and my professional life, I see periods when it seemed that I was making little or no progress. In fact, there were times when I seemed to be moving backward. Yet without exception the times when I moved forward the fastest were the times when I received new information and acted on it. It is my hope and prayer that the information in this book will be such a catapult for you.

WHY USE PERSONALITY PROFILING AT WORK?

Life is hard. And business is even harder. Working in the business world today has been compared to having to change a flat tire while the car is moving ninety miles an hour.

Management books are full of theories—some simple, many complex—on how to get the most performance out of employees and associates. As I was preparing to do research for this book, I went

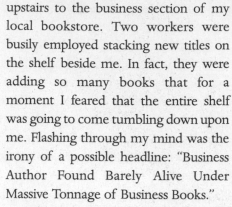

WORKING IN THE
BUSINESS WORLD
TODAY HAS BEEN
COMPARED TO
HAVING TO
CHANGE A FLAT
TIRE WHILE THE
CAR IS MOVING
NINETY MILES
AN HOUR.

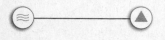

upstairs to the business section of my local bookstore. Two workers were busily employed stacking new titles on the shelf beside me. In fact, they were adding so many books that for a moment I feared that the entire shelf was going to come tumbling down upon me. Flashing through my mind was the irony of a possible headline: "Business Author Found Barely Alive Under Massive Tonnage of Business Books."

I also thought about my recent work with a Fortune 100 company. The leadership team ruefully handed me the newest boss's manifesto, a document at least four inches thick. "This is the latest from our newest vice president," one of them observed. "He's calling it the Emerging Leaders Program. We have another name for it," he said, pointing to the stack of other documents on leadership he was supposed to read—from the former vice president who left six months ago.

"What is that?" I asked him.

"We call it the Submerging Leaders Program. Every new executive wants to make his mark on us, and we can barely keep up with the day-to-day activities we need to do to keep this ship afloat while the leadership marches on and off."

According to *Fast Company* magazine, the number one thing that keeps CEOs up at night is "keeping up with the latest trends" (Ed. John Byrne, August 2004). It is no wonder that the search is on for some new tool or strategy that will give them an edge in the ever more competitive global market. The rate of business failures is abysmally high. Fewer than two in ten start-up companies will survive the first five years. And the big companies that are established don't have it so easy either.

Markets are changing at the speed of light, causing the monoliths to have to guard existing customer bases even as they try to fend off potential garage-kid geniuses coming up with new ideas. Whoever thought that a company named Google could turn two twenty-year-olds into billionaires? Whoever thought that AT&T, the one-time leading telephone carrier, would be sold off in parts due to its inability to keep up with the changing times?

"Uneasy lies the head that wears a crown," Shakespeare's King Henry IV observed, and no CEO that I know is patting him or herself on the back declaring all is well in the kingdom. Constant vigilance, matched with the need for constant innovation and ever-increasing profitability, makes business leadership one of the most stressful occupations today.

Things ain't so easy for the little guys and gals either. In 2002 more than twenty thousand companies laid off at least one hundred workers each.[1] In fact, more Americans have experienced being laid off than have experienced being the victims of violent crime. For some workers, the wounds are the same. An article in the *MIT Sloan Management Review* called "A Study of Spirituality in the Workplace" reported that the majority of workers surveyed said they had experienced a "wounding of the soul" at work.[2] And that's just the part you can't see.

In (not so) merry England, dissatisfaction reigns. An article in *Automotive Management* magazine, "We Like 40% of Our Staff," reported that a 1999 survey of more than one thousand human resource directors in British companies declared that 60 percent of the staff are so poorly engaged that most employers would not rehire them. And nearly a quarter of those survey respondents, writes Jeffrey Oxman in "The Hidden Leverage of Human Capital," did not believe that their workforce gave their companies a competitive edge.[3]

Authors John Izzo and Pam Withers point out in their seminal book *Values Shift* that much of the management and leadership that is taking place today is actually "reparenting." Latchkey kids who were left alone after school both spurn and want authority. Baby boomers who regarded work as the reason to live are now coming to terms with maybe not working so hard after all. New hires coming up through the ranks of colleges all too often need basic remedial writing and math skills due to an educational system that for a while took "Pass/Fail" to a whole new level—or depth.

CHIHUAHUAS DON'T LIKE WATER

In all of this, one thing remains clear. We are different. And while diversity programs abound, the emphasis on differences in race, age, and gender overlook perhaps the most basic fact of human diversity: personality. Personality-driven behavior dictates actions, and actions determine success or failure, harmony or riot, in any and every endeavor.

Understanding the elements of Earth, Water, Wind, and Fire is a means of determining individual and team behavioral tendencies that affect everything from career choice to daily "to do" lists. *We choose to act on what we value, and each element values very different things.*

For example, Fire personalities thrive in atmospheres of challenge and confrontation, while Water personalities thrive with harmony and calm. Wind personality types love chaos and change, while Earth personality types crave order and structure. Needless to say, "challenge the boss" might be high on a Fire's "to do" list, but it's never on a Water's list. "Organize files" would probably be the very first order of business for an Earth, but it would be nonexistent on a Wind's list.

TRY GETTING A CHIHUAHUA TO LEAP INTO WATER . . . AND YOU HAVE A PICTURE OF TASK ASSIGNMENT RESISTANCE THAT MANY MANAGERS AND LEADERS FACE ON A DAILY BASIS.

Yet every day people are assigned tasks based on job descriptions that have little or no bearing on their talents and natural personality types. The result is that teams are struggling with unnecessary heavy lifting. If the elemental makeup of each team member were understood, however, tasks could be done much more efficiently and quickly, with team members loving their work and feeling that it is even more like play.

Just observe a Labrador retriever trembling with desire to leap into the water and fetch a stick. If you were able to ask the dog afterward if it was "hard work," the Labrador would say, "Work? What work? That was fun!" Try getting a Chihuahua to leap into water, however, and you have a picture of task-assignment resistance that many managers and leaders face on a daily basis.

A dog is a dog is a dog, right? Wrong. Different breeds love different things. It is the same with people. The personality's hard wiring is the lens through which we view the world. It is our way of being "smart," and it ultimately affects how we see the world and how others see us.

The article "Typed and Transformed" in the May–June 2004 issue of *Utne* magazine had the subtitle "Personality typing isn't exactly psychology—it's something better." In it author and senior editor Jon Spayde admitted that he had come to the conclusion in graduate school that there were basically two types of people: those who were smart and those who were not.

He went on to explain that as he matured and learned more about the different personality types in the world, he had a new perspective on colleagues, especially those in meetings. He also included a fascinating perspective worth reviewing. It seems that Sigmund Freud was an extrovert, and Alfred Adler was an introvert; Carl Jung, who knew both men, was able to observe the differences in their psychological perspectives and writings. (Freud believed everything stemmed from sexual or outward preoccupations, while Adler believed that everything stemmed from one's attempt to protect oneself from the outer world.)

Learning to think like another element doesn't come easily. Some have compared it to trying to teach a right-handed person to use the left hand. Yet new ways of thinking and relating to others can be taught, and once it is, the results can be astounding. The scientists' innate personality differences shaped how they viewed the world at large. It is the same with you and me.

For example, I worked with a sales team that kept meeting with resistance from purchasing agents. When the team realized that they were Wind and the agents were Earth, they shifted their approach from using words such as *change, fast, speed, new,* and *different* (Wind words) to *systematic, improvements, performance, longevity,* and *reliability* (Earth words). Orders increased tenfold.

Using the Elements in Business Hiring

At one time a prospective employer could place a call to a previous employer and get a quick and candid overview of the potential employee's skills, but those days are gone. Litigation and strict rules about what can and cannot be said about someone have limited the ways that employers can get solid information about a person's performance in the workplace.

Making a poor match in the workplace can cost thousands of dollars in lost revenue, new recruiting and hiring expenses, and training costs. According to an article by Shelly Doll at Builder.com, "Using personality tests can help people reduce the risk of incorrectly judging a potential employee's character, and may help you better understand your staff's motivations and actions."

Today more and more CEOs are using personality assessment tools to better understand and manage employees that they already have or are thinking of hiring. In a June 2004 issue of *Inc.* magazine, the story is told of Alpine Confections, one of the largest candy makers in North America, turning to personality assessments to help their team prioritize more effectively. The result? Two major acquisitions in the past two years and a major licensing agreement with Hallmark. CEO David Taiclet claims that the assessment "illuminated some of our management tendencies, and our confidence level definitely increased as a result."

Overall employment testing, including personality testing, has been growing at a rate of ten to fifteen percent a year in the past three years, according to the Association of Test Publishers.[4] Companies ranging from FedEx to Chick-Fil-A, the WNBA's Phoenix Mercury, and the Chicago Cubs have been using personality tests and assessments to help them find proper fits for their team as well as increase the productivity of each employee. The truth is, teams are comprised of highly diverse personality types, many of whom can easily be in conflict if their differences are not understood, respected, and valued.

Anyone who plays the game of chess knows that each piece is uniquely suited for a particular kind of move and strategy. Yet too many organizations consider the game as being made up of only kings and pawns. Life and work are much more complex and intricately balanced than that, and a wise strategist would know the powers of each piece on the board, especially his or her own.

It is my hope that the presentation and understanding of this material will equip individuals in all walks of life to more effectively interact with others, leading to win-win strategies for all.

PART 1

Learning the Elements

UNDERSTANDING THE ELEMENTS: WHICH ONE ARE YOU?

Earth. Water. Wind. Fire. Which one are you? And what does it matter? This book will help to educate and convince you that knowing the difference is important indeed. And it will also help you take this individual tool of the Path Elements Profile™ (PEP) and expand it into a team assessment that can help transform not one, but many individuals into a harmonizing, humming force for good.

It is imperative that leaders first understand their own elements in order to assess their strengths and challenges.

One CEO I was coaching, for example, is an inventor—and a certifiable genius—from the Silicon Valley. However, he had burned through six assistants in a year, blaming each one of them for their failures. Only when he saw his element, Fire, and understood his current and most willing assistant, Water, did he realize that his flame was not giving as much light as heat. He was on the verge of accomplishing nothing of worth without a team that understood him and, more important, that he understood and respected. Are you a Fire burning through your team, or perhaps another element with its own unique set of strengths and challenges? Let's find out now.

IDENTIFYING THE POSITIVE
CHARACTERISTICS OF EACH ELEMENT

In this section, please take the time to contemplate each of the four elements. These activities are designed to trigger new synapses in your brain and create a new mind map for you to better reference and absorb the information that will follow.

What are the unique and positive characteristics of each of the elements? All are powerful. All are beautiful. All can be dangerous when unharnessed or out of control. Yet for our purposes here let's consider the positive characteristics of each element.

- Quickly name five positive characteristics of Earth and write them here:

  Earth is/does . . .

  1. solid
  2. *Foundation*
  3. *nutrients (plants / food)*
  4. *round / never ending*
  5. *Clay*

- Name five positive characteristics of Water and write them here:

  Water is/does . . .

  1. transparent
  2. *Calming*
  3. *Hydrating*
  4. *wavy*
  5. *healing for muscles*

- Now name five positive characteristics of Wind and write them here:

  Wind is/does . . .

  1. invisible
  2. *Cooling / breezy*
  3. *Soothing*
  4. *threatening / powerful*
  5. *whirlwind - energy*

- Name five positive characteristic of Fire and write them here:

  Fire is/does . . .

  1. all-consuming
  2. *Heat / hot*
  3. *purifying*
  4. *Colorful*
  5. *Mesmerizing*

- Now quickly choose the element you most relate to and write it here:

  I feel most like *wind*.

  If you are torn between two elements, write both of them here:

  I feel I may be a blend of *wind* and *fire*.

If you are uncertain, ask family, friends, and coworkers to choose for you. They usually can identify your elements.

PICTURE A QUADRANT.

Deliberate	Fast
People	Results

At the top of the quadrant are the words *Deliberate* and *Fast*. Place a dot in the quadrant that is most like you.

At the bottom of the quadrant are the words *People* and *Results*. Place a dot in the quadrant that most attracts you.

> If you placed yourself in the Deliberate quadrant, you tend toward Earth.
> If you placed yourself in the Fast quadrant, you tend toward Wind.
> If you placed yourself in the People quadrant, you tend toward Water.
> If you placed yourself in the Results quadrant, you tend toward Fire.

Now look at your two dots. Where they are may be a reflection of your personality blend. For example, if you are in the Fast quadrant and the People quadrant, you are probably a Wind/Water. If you are in the Deliberate quadrant and the Results quadrant, you may be an Earth/Fire.

Another guide is to read the following statements and circle your answer to each one.

- People say I make decisions quickly, often based on just the "scent" of something. True or False
  (If you answered True, your tendency is toward Wind.)
- When it comes to choosing between people or results, I have to admit I almost always put people first. True or False
  (If you answered True, your tendency is toward Water.)
- When it comes to decision making, I prefer to move based on evidence. True or False
  (If you answered True, your tendency is toward Earth.)
- Once I commit to something, I give 110 percent to the task and am often angry when others don't do the same. True or False
  (If you answered True, your tendency is toward Fire.)

If you would like to have more information about taking the full PEP test, please go to my Web site, www.lauriebethjones.com, or see the information page at the end of this book.

Before we had the PEP online assessment, which pinpoints accurately each person's elemental makeup, I thought I was Water. I wanted to be Water, mostly because Jesus said He was "Living Water," but also because Water is beautifully capable of changing form.

However, my friends unanimously told me I was Wind and Fire, which gave me a whole new insight into how I was behaving in my relationships as well as in my calling. Even though I didn't get to be Living Water like Jesus, I took comfort when one friend reminded me that the Holy Spirit is compared to Wind and Fire in Scripture.

So, my dominant elements are Wind and Fire, with a little bit of Water and hardly any Earth. Therefore, I love to message with results, but am not too good at nurturing or details. This profile has proven challenging in my career choices and relationships. (My former bosses have openly shared that I was basically not a very good "employee.") Once I got who I was, however, as a self-directed author and speaker, I began to lead with my strengths and "team" for my challenges. (You may view my PEP report in Appendix II.)

I strongly urge you to pause here and, before you continue, get feedback from friends and family about how they see you in elemental terms. The insights you gain about your behaviors and their perceptions of you will be worth the price of this book. By capturing your essence in terms of Earth, Water, Wind, or Fire, people can communicate your strengths as well as your challenges in nonjudgmental, loving, insightful, and often humorous ways.

In one seminar I conducted in Seattle, a gentleman named Jackson expressed his inner uncertainty. His team unanimously called out, "Jackson, you are Wind!" amid great howls of laughter. Sometimes we see ourselves through a glass darkly, while those around us can see quite clearly.

Stop here and get feedback from your friends and family.

UNDERSTANDING PERSONALITY BLENDS

There are sixteen possible personality blends:

Earth	Water
Earth/Wind	Water/Wind
Earth/Water	Water/Earth
Earth/Fire	Water/Fire

Wind	Fire
Wind/Water	Fire/Wind
Wind/Earth	Fire/Earth
Wind/Fire	Fire/Water

I have developed symbols for each one of these, which are as follows:

Almost 3 percent of the population will be fusions. They will be about evenly matched in all the elements. Because they are capable of changing form as needed, I typically relate fusions to the Water element for purposes of discussion.

The value of having the full overview of your elemental makeup is discovering where you are strong and where you are challenged. The implication of this self-knowledge is profound and far-reaching. It can and will affect (and has been affecting) everything from your relationships to your career choices, leadership style, and happiness needs.

Your personality type influences you in each of the following areas. In this section I will detail each area for the basic elements of Earth, Water, Wind, and Fire.

Action	Adventure	Anger
Authority	Change	Communication
Conflict	Fears	Fun
Ideal Work Environment	Leadership	Learning
	Order	Pace
Leisure	Stress	Success
Relationships	Tasks	

Now that you have made a quick guess and/or gotten feedback from others about your elemental makeup, let's look at the elements in more depth.

EARTH

Earth is "terra firma" for us. It is the foundation of everything we do. It is our home, our grounding point, our anchor. It is steady and solid. Earth is predictable in its seasons and cycles and rotations. It is perfectly poised and balanced at all times, and is magnificent in its diversity. It supports all life forms and is equally comfortable and at work whether it is winter, summer, spring, or fall. Earth stores and saves and works silently and steadily to maintain diverse forms of life. It seeks balance and sustainability in all things. It is rich, fertile, vast, and full of resources.

Earth is also generous, nourishing, supportive, ordered, and colorful. It has multiple textures and incredible depths. It can be towering and sheltering, dynamic and peaceful. It is slow to change, fertile, and full of treasures. Earth is aware of the "gravity" of every situation and operates on predictable laws. Earth knows that everything "matters." You can almost always count on earth to be there, no matter what.

Name other positive characteristics of earth that come to mind for you, and write them on a piece of paper or in a notebook. Participants in my Path seminars have added the following words to the list for earth:

abundant	active	balanced
beautiful	changing	colorful
comforting	communal	consistent
deep	diverse	dynamic
earthy	evolving	experienced
fertile	foundational	fruitful
generous	gravitating	grounded

healing	home	life-bearing
multifaceted	multilayered	nourishing
nurturing	ordered	oriented
peaceful	powerful	precious
regenerative	reliable	resourceful
restorative	rich	sacred
sheltering	slow to change	solid
spinning	stable	supportive
sustaining	textural	towering
transformative	treasureful	vast
warm		

WATER

Water is the most vital and necessary of all the elements. Without water, nothing lives. It is fluid, cleansing, life-giving, shape-shifting, expansive, pure, and sculpting. It is tranquil, reflective, transparent, shimmering, clear, and nourishing. Water is deep, irresistible, dramatic, sparkling, entertaining, singing, still, and healing. Water is capable of changing form into ice or snow or mist or rain. It is flexible, taking the shape of whatever it is poured into. It is a solvent, dissolving hard substances and making things easier to swallow. It is capable of diluting solids. It is patient, taking eons to sculpt canyons as it quietly moves along. It is renewing and inspiring. Water takes the path of least resistance and "goes with the flow." It is easily directed and pours itself 100 percent into whatever it does, wherever it is.

Water is very comfortable with change and works silently and invisibly to nurture and sustain life. Name other characteristics of water, and write them in your notebook. Here are more words to describe water:

bubbly	buoyant	calming
cleansing	clear	cooling
deep	detoxifying	dramatic

energizing	entertaining	essential
ever-changing	expansive	flowing
fluid	form-changing	freeing
fun-filled	healing	holding
immutable	intoxicating	irresistible
life-bearing	life-giving	luxurious
magnifying	mesmerizing	noisy
nourishing	powerful	pure
quenching	reflective	refreshing
rhythmic	sculpting	serene
shape-shifting	shimmering	singing
solid	soothing	sparkling
still	surging	tranquil
transforming	transparent	transporting
vital		

WIND

Wind is swift, uplifting, whirling, motion oriented, and refreshing. It can be silent or howling, and is itself invisible. It is mysterious, unpredictable, energetic, and global. It is cleansing, musical, electric, haunting, sweeping, caressing, and scent-bearing. Wind warns, cools, soothes, and pollinates. It inspires, literally giving "breath" to everything that moves. Wind can penetrate through cracks and walls and fabric. It is persuasive and enigmatic. It can whisper and caress and tease and play. It can lift up kites and dash down buildings. It supports butterflies and hummingbirds and can sweep the old away in a single breath. Name other characteristics of wind, and write them in your notebook. The following list describes wind:

boundless	caressing	changeable
cleansing	confident	cooling
creative	dynamic	electric

eliminating	enabling	energetic
enigmatic	exciting	forceful
freeing	fun	gentle
global	God-breathed	haunting
howling	invisible	lyrical
mesmerizing	moody	motion-directed
multidirectional	musical	mysterious
necessary	omniscient	penetrating
persuasive	pollinating	powerful
prevailing	refreshing	scent-bearing
seed-bearing	silent	soothing
strong	sweeping	swift
temporary	unpredictable	untamed
uplifting	warning	whirling
whispering	wild	

FIRE

Fire is purifying, hot, illuminating, and passionate. It is dancing, sizzling, radiant, freeing, and captivating. It ignites, comforts, signals, blazes, and roars. It is romantic, wild, hungry, and intense. It is insatiable, transformational, and contagious. It can be cozy, glowing, and civilizing. It gives warmth and light, and keeps away the wild beasts. It also stirs up what is wild within us. Fire is useful, regenerating, consuming, and motivating. It is energizing, forging, purifying, and renewing. Write other positive characteristics of fire in your notebook. Here are more words to describe fire:

attractive	blazing	brilliant
captivating	catalytic	changeable
civilizing	cleansing	colorful
comforting	communicative	consuming
cozy	dancing	energizing
fascinating	forging	freeing

13

glowing	has no boundaries	hot
hungry	igniting	illuminating
insatiable	inspiring	intense
joyful	life-sustaining	light
lingering	mesmerizing	motivating
passionate	playful	powerful
purifying	radiant	regenerating
renewing	restoring	roaring
romantic	sense of home	signaling
sizzling	spreading	transformational
unpredictable	unstoppable	useful
warm	wild	

GOING DEEPER

Now let's consider strengths, challenges, likes, and dislikes of each element.

EARTH

Earth's strengths include stability, predictability, a sense of the long term, grounding, and orderly movement. Earth is sure of itself.

Earth's challenges include a tendency to be stubborn, being unyielding and locked into old ways of doing things, and an unwillingness to move. Earth can be boring without the other elements.

Earth likes structure, stability, long-term thinking, commitment, being asked for sound advice, planning deadlines that are adhered to, details and facts, and regular and constant communication ("I need you to touch base with me on this," or "E.T., phone home").

Earth dislikes sudden movement, words like *new* or *radical* or *change*, things that are "different," too much spontaneity, sudden changes in plans, chaos or clutter, and unpredictability.

Meditation for Earth

I am Earth.
I give soil and substance
  to those around me.
I support and protect all
  living things.
I guard resources so life
  may be sustained in all
  seasons.
I am sure.
I am steady. I am Firm.
I am Earth.

I do best when given facts, data, information, and time to process and create in an unhurried, orderly fashion.

Shadow Side of Earth

Others sometimes see me as . . .
boring
stubborn
hardhearted
dense
slow to move
stuck in the mud
picky
obsessive about order or details

To bring more balance, I need to open up to new ideas and be more willing to take risks.

EARTH TENDENCIES

Action

Earth prefers to gather information and move cautiously. Wants assurance of a desired outcome before taking action. Tends to be better at maintaining and completing rather than starting.

Adventure

Earth respects consequences and seeks safety over risk. Prefers to choose a planned activity over an impromptu experience. Typically has a backup plan and wants to be prepared for unexpected events.

Anger

Earth does not welcome showy displays of emotion, and views loss of self-control as a sign of immaturity and weakness. Can become irritated or even angry about careless inattention to details, inconsistency, and hypocrisy.

Authority

Earth respects authority because of its need for order and balance but will resist authority that demands ethical or legal compromise. Tends to know and live by rules, and enforces boundaries in its work and personal relationships.

Change

Earth usually changes slowly. Is very concerned about accuracy and is quick to notice errors, so its first response is that change creates many mistakes that must be corrected. Tends to value experience over ideas, but will promote change that improves efficiency and correctness.

Communication

Earth thinks through ideas before speaking and listens objectively to others' statements. Tends to clarify —"tell," not "sell"—and does not exaggerate to make a point. Wants facts backed up by data and logic. Relies on written or verbal, not physical, communication.

Conflict

Earth defends its high standards but prefers avoiding confrontation or emotional situations if possible. Uses measured reason and logic, and counterattacks using details to point out others' inconsistencies. May give in and then work behind the scenes to validate its viewpoint.

Fears

Earth's greatest fears are making mistakes, taking uncertain risks, and encountering unpredictable outcomes. Perfection and security are concerns that may cause Earths to overanalyze and miss short-term opportunities.

Fun

Earth prefers activities that have a purpose. Often, hobbies and interests involve collecting things or gaining knowledge in special interests. Enjoys solo or small group activities.

Ideal Work Environment

Earth wants to be rewarded for producing quality. Prefers to work quietly, alone, or in a small group. Work space is usually functional, impersonal, and neat—with charts, graphs, and filing/storage systems. Enjoys working with others who value accuracy, foresight, and planning. Seeks clearly defined roles and responsibilities, with ability to complete projects according to plan and schedule.

Leadership

Earth leads by example, based on principles and standards, with a long-term view. Good at developing systems and processes that eliminate crisis management and chaos. Does not respond well to emotional, undisciplined leadership.

Learning

Earth has a strong sense of curiosity. Can become more interested in understanding theories than in making practical use of its knowledge. Learns well in structured environments with specific objectives, detailed questions, and measurable outcomes. Wants to learn the right way.

Leisure

Earth enjoys solitude and seeks quiet time alone with its thoughts. May especially enjoy reading. Devotes time to self-improvement and personal discipline. Does not like to be idle and may enjoy working with hands.

Order

Earth is orderly by nature, seeking "a place for everything, and everything in its place." Organizes information for efficient use and identifies systems, patterns, categories, details, and methods. Tends to prefer neat and tidy surroundings.

Pace

Earth tends to operate at a measured and steady pace. Like our planet that rotates imperceptibly at a thousand miles an hour, people with this style can make steady, predictable progress toward their goal without being noticed.

Relationships

Earth does not trust readily or easily but is capable of developing deep and lasting friendships. Builds quality relationships over time, based on demonstrated integrity and mutual respect. Expects and gives loyalty.

Stress

Earth can become stressed by disorder, chaos, and concerns about the unknown. There is a strong need to have clear goals, order, and time to plan and verify, while avoiding impulsive decisions and spontaneous actions. Tends not to discuss its worries but frets quietly. Becomes cold and distant when stressed.

Success

Earth views success with a long-term perspective and tends to think and operate generationally. Understands that worthwhile achievements require sacrifice and is suspicious of something-for-nothing opportunities. Tends to be self-critical.

Tasks

Earth prefers specific duties and procedures, working with a high degree of accuracy. Excels in quality control and is attentive to detail. Brings improved organization and efficiency to its projects. Plans carefully and thoroughly before beginning work.

WATER

Water's strengths include its vitality, life-giving properties, flexibility, and easygoing nature. It brings balance, is a problem solver, finds solutions, seeks harmony, and is a team player.

Water's challenges include its tendency to quickly lose its identity in others and to absorb without discrimination the good and the bad. It has difficulty saying no. It is a people pleaser, can become stagnant without an outlet, and takes on the toxins around it.

Water likes feeling needed, time for reflection, certain boundaries, working behind the scenes, bringing life and harmony to situations, and the challenges of life.

Water dislikes stubbornness, inflexibility, lack of clarity, imbalance, rigid thinking, and moving uphill.

MEDITATION FOR WATER

I am Water.
I am flowing and refreshing,
Life-giving and clear.
I am essential, dynamic, and transparent.
I adapt easily to different forms.
I go under, over, around, and through whatever
obstacle is placed before me.
I am loyal, patient, and supportive.
I give life wherever I go.

I do best when given solid boundaries, clear expectations and guidance, and defined forms to fill. I also want freedom to determine my own way to the goal, and I require lots of patience for my work to do its work.

SHADOW SIDE OF WATER

Sometimes others see me as . . .
unstable
slow
easily polluted
unwilling to take a stand
unreliable
procrastinating
wishy-washy
valuing feelings over results
silent

To bring more balance, I need to be unafraid of confrontation and willing to speak up for myself.

WATER TENDENCIES

Action

Water is slow to take action, preferring to understand expectations and move carefully. Wants clear explanations and will probably return for clarifications while taking action. Prefers to be a responder instead of an initiator. Tends to be better at finishing rather than starting projects.

Adventure

Water prefers predictability and resists change. Does not welcome surprises but will usually go along as a team player. Is not energized by challenging situations and may need quiet time to recharge.

Anger

Waters tend to stuff feelings of anger and resentment, so it can be difficult to detect when they are angry. Their long fuse burns slowly, but when they reach their limit, they may release all their pent-up emotions on the individual who has finally exhausted their patience.

Authority

Waters tend to defer to authority, in large part because they are not highly motivated to exercise authority and wield power. Rather than oppose leaders openly, Waters may "do it their own way" while fulfilling duties. Follow rules that make sense and are time-proven.

Change

Water prefers predictability and may be slow to accept change. Needs ample warning and preparation time whenever change is introduced.

Communication

Water usually is a good listener, and this quality helps others communicate and understand more clearly. Usually shares openly with very close friends—may even be talkative in those situations. Doesn't voice opposition comfortably and may not speak up in meetings.

Conflict

Water responds to conflict between individuals by trying to restore harmony and bring agreement. Response to interpersonal conflict is usually fleeing or giving in. A tendency toward passive-aggressive behavior means Water deals with disagreement indirectly while appearing to give support.

Fears

Water's greatest fears involve confrontation, conflict, and change. The safety of predictable routines is reassuring, and fear of the unknown may be immobilizing at times. May not express fears to others.

Fun

Team sports may have the most appeal for Water because it's about winning together. Games, leisure activities, and time with family and friends can also be sources of enjoyment.

Ideal Work Environment

Water can excel in a variety of work environments as long as harmony and stability exist. Prefers easygoing leadership, settled surroundings, established methods, predictable assignments, unhurried time frames, and close teamwork. Welcoming, personal touches are evident in work space furnishings and decorations—homelike, with photos and mementos of family and friends.

Leadership

Water emphasizes inclusion and consensus; encourages cooperation rather than enforcing compliance. Wins loyalty through commitment to and support of others.

Learning

Water prefers to see practical application of information to specific situations. Prefers using reliable, traditional methods over learning innovative, new techniques.

Leisure

Water enjoys quiet times with close friends, movies, books, and "nothing" times that include naps, passive relaxation, and even hot baths. May enjoy offering hospitality at home, or volunteering for charity work.

Order

Waters support orderliness while seeking stability but can have difficulty establishing priorities—neatness and organization are not necessarily their driving motivations. Instead, practicality and predictability determine the need for order and balance in their lives.

Pace

Water tends to operate at a steady pace according to an internal clock rather than external demands. When feeling pressure to speed up, Water may slow down or even lock down in response. Prefers to concentrate on one project at a time and see it through to completion.

Relationships

Water accepts others openly but may not reach out naturally to begin relationships. People-oriented and generous in many ways, Water enjoys helping others succeed.

Stress

Water is stressed by disharmony, change, loud and boisterous activities, and conflict. Feeling unappreciated or being taken for granted can become stressful. Trying to meet everyone's expectations and masking emotions are two factors that contribute to Water's anxiety.

Success

Water views success in terms of how it has helped others succeed. Similarly, having fulfilling relationships is viewed as a rewarding achievement. While appreciating acknowledgment for contributions, Water does not want to be singled out for attention, is easily embarrassed by public acclaim, and prefers personal and more private recognition.

Tasks

Water is very versatile and works well with tasks and people. Wants to see everyone's needs addressed when accomplishing a task. Completes tasks others start and wants closure before beginning another one. Tends to be very thorough and persistent in meeting expectations.

WIND

Wind's strengths include spontaneity, energy, forward motion, and the ability to supersede all boundaries. It is the element most capable of moving all others. It the first element to bring the scent of danger, and it is the first element to bring the scent of spring.

Wind's challenges include restlessness, unpredictability, and impulsiveness. It loves to stir things up and then leave. It is invisible and hard to pin down. It doesn't weigh the consequences of its actions, and it has trouble following through and focusing for long periods of time.

Wind likes change, ideas, foretelling trends, uplifting and inspiring things, motion in multiple directions, possibilities, blue sky, and limitless thinking.

Wind dislikes lack of responsiveness, routine, a narrow focus, responsibility, staying in one place, predictability, and deadlines.

MEDITATION FOR WIND

I am Wind.
I am invisible, uplifting, and powerful.
I influence, direct, and soothe.
I am inspirational and energizing.
I am a messenger.
I circle the globe and see all.
I am forever in motion, seeing fun and life and action.
I think and act spontaneously.
I love being around others.
I follow my instincts and the scent of things.

I do best when I am given encouragement, responsiveness, detailed ground support, trust, and room to move.

SHADOW SIDE OF WIND

Others sometimes see me as . . .
unstable
unpredictable
disorganized
unfocused
impulsive
restless
flighty
loud
demanding
unrelenting
misdirected

To bring balance, I need to be more willing to commit to a direction and follow through.

WIND TENDENCIES

Action

Wind enjoys being on the move and loves activity of almost any kind. Can sometimes be quick and impulsive when taking action— and tends to "kick up dust." Tends to think out loud in order to solve problems. Sometimes mistakes talking for doing and feelings for results.

Adventure

Wind tends to expect positive outcomes and usually feels unthreatened by unpredictable results. Winds place great faith in natural charm and verbal persuasion skills; expect to "talk their way out" of any challenging circumstance—and often do!

Anger

Wind may be quick to speak in anger and may use words regretted later. Tends to "explode" and then forgive and restore relationships quickly. Wants to talk through causes of anger. Cause of anger is often injured pride; may shift blame to others in order to look good.

Authority

Winds' strong desire for freedom may cause them to be casual about authority and rules. When words or actions provoke an unintended response, may react with humor, trying to ease tension. Tend to view and approach others as peers instead of recognizing formal lines of authority.

Communication

Wind verbalizes feelings and arrives at decisions by talking issues out. Listening skills are generally not highly developed. Communicates and influences through persuasive appeals, stories, and humor. Is usually unguarded in conversation; may exaggerate; may display emotions openly.

Conflict

Wind diffuses tension through humor. May joke about or trivialize a serious situation to avoid responsibility and consequences. Can be seen as self-promoting or manipulative. May take things personally and attack the integrity or character of others.

Fears

Wind's greatest fear is social rejection and isolation. Tends to perform for admiration and approval. Needs reassurances of acceptance. Fears loss of influence and wants to be taken seriously and regarded as credible.

Fun

Wind prefers variety and spontaneity. Enjoys time with people, centered on activities; tends to do well in large groups. Bored by repetition; seeks sensory experiences: eating, playing, joking, laughing, touching. Enjoys unique experiences that can be talked about later.

Ideal Work Environment

Wind wants to be around people who are friendly and responsive. Prefers a leader who is sociable and offers short-term incentives with frequent feedback opportunities. Enjoys working on challenging, people-centered issues requiring interaction. Needs freedom from lengthy, detailed reports, whether writing or reading them. Also needs physical activity instead of sitting most of the time.

Leadership

Wind prefers not to be a detail-oriented leader and does not respond well to a leader who is authoritarian or unsociable. Inspires and socializes as a means of motivation. Seeks out willing participants. Tends to have an open-door policy. Makes promises willingly; is distracted easily.

Learning

Wind learns by doing, in a relaxed atmosphere. Learns best where there is personal contact allowing for approval and affirmation. Likes stories that teach. Tends not to connect abstract concepts unrelated to real-life situations. Applies learning within the context of social outcomes. Learns through variety, interaction, and games.

Leisure

Wind enjoys spending time with others and seeks out companions for spontaneous activities. Tends to be restless and does not like sitting around. Leisure activities need not have a focus as long as they involve people, places, and changing scenery.

Order

Wind is disorganized by nature and tends to put things in piles rather than place them in files. Prioritizes according to urgency instead of purpose and often puts off projects until the deadline. Tends to spread out when working and may have many simultaneous projects and activities.

Relationships

Wind does not discriminate in making friends—may value the quantity of relationships as much or more than quality. Tends to trust easily and forgive quickly. Wants to be judged by intentions when neglectful in relationships.

Stress

Wind becomes stressed by isolation, social rejection, loss of influence, and repetitive activities. Feels a strong need to interact with others. Self-worth is determined by external circumstances.

Success

Wind views success in terms of popularity, status, and access to people. Tends to apply energies to achieving short-term successes that lead to public recognition. Motivated by immediate rewards. May give up before succeeding if not encouraged and reinforced.

Tasks

Wind works best with people and prefers to have fun while working. Often devises a game that makes work more recreational. May not be objective in evaluating its own work. Views criticism of results as personal rejection. May start enthusiastically but lose interest or energy quickly unless others are alongside.

Fire

Fire's strengths include being mesmerizing, exciting, passionate, intense, purifying, illuminating, and committed. It has no fear of confrontation.

Fire's challenges include the tendency to burn out quickly and the inability to set its own boundaries. It can destroy as well as purify, it may lack social skills, it may be unbalanced, and it may be insensitive to others' needs and weaknesses. It has no fear of confrontation.

Fire likes fuel, excitement, heat, pressure, constant tending and stoking, entertaining others, oxygen and new possibilities, action, and change.

Fire dislikes boredom, sameness, routine, the past (there is no fuel in ashes), slow-moving or lukewarm people, boundaries, sharing the spotlight, and apathy.

Meditation for Fire

I am Fire.
I am hot, mesmerizing, passionate.
I am courageous and bold.
I confront and refine,
Purify and reform whatever I encounter.

I shed light as well as heat.
I am civilizing, power generating,
Decisive and sure.
I am colorful, lively, transforming, and inviting.
I commit 110 percent of my being to whatever task is before me.
I am visionary and results oriented.
I cause things to happen.

I do best when I am given challenges, acknowledgment, time, and the freedom to act and be in control.

SHADOW SIDE OF FIRE

Others sometimes see me as . . .
destructive
uncontrollable
hot
dominating
frightening
self-centered
combative
judgmental
insensitive
intense
all-consuming

To bring more balance, I need to listen more to others and share the glory.

FIRE TENDENCIES

Action
Fire is quick to take action. Making decisions and then acting quickly is a way of life. Frequently has many projects going at once.

Tends to meet difficult challenges with massive action and expects the same level of action and commitment from others who are involved.

Adventure

Fire enjoys adventure because of a drive to conquer challenges and be in control. Sets goals in concrete and plans to reach them in sand—expects to conquer obstacles and is seldom intimidated by the unexpected.

Anger

Fire displays anger as its primary emotion. This intensity intimidates others who view them as "too hot to handle" at times. Response to anger from others is met by even more anger—the desire to win at any cost often overpowers more controlled means of expression.

Authority

Fire likes to set the rules and may disregard outside rules. Has a temptation toward "the end justifies the means" thinking. Assumes control and takes charge instinctively. Boldness may be perceived as arrogance; confrontational in disagreements. Recognizes and respects power and has difficulty submitting to others who seem less certain.

Communication

Fire wants the bottom line first. Prefers high points and facts presented in bullet form and will ask for details if they seem important. Reveals information on a need-to-know basis as a way of maintaining control. Speaks directly to issues and results; makes flat statements.

Conflict

Fire enjoys conflict and sees it as necessary for staying red-hot and burning brightly. Resists opposition and expects to win; becomes aggressive in overcoming objections. May respect opposition as a demonstration of commitment and courage.

Fears

Fire's greatest fears are losing control, being seen as vulnerable or ineffective, and loss of prestige. Fears being "ordinary"—sets high objectives and expects rewards for personal and professional accomplishments.

Fun

Fire isn't seen as fun-oriented because of commitment to high achievement. *Workaholic* is a term often applied, although competition is a source of enjoyment. Often individualistic. Wants to be the leader if involved in team sports, but may prefer meeting personal challenges.

Ideal Work Environment

Fires want rewards for results, freedom from routine and repetitive tasks, opportunities to innovate and direct, and administrative support to release them from details that drain their energy. Seek leadership and a challenge worthy of conquering. Need to choose direction and strategy. Work where feedback and opinions count, where "ownership" is part of responsibility, and where commitment is solid.

Leadership

Fire is strong-willed and tends to view leadership as imposing will on others. Has a small inner circle of advisors and keeps workers on the outside. Sees the big picture and delegates responsibilities. Responds to leadership that is direct, challenging, goal-oriented and rewards accomplishment.

Learning

Fire would rather be the teacher than the student. Wants to know enough to succeed but leaves details to subordinates. More eager to apply information than learn and understand it thoroughly—may infer other meanings and take action based on a faulty understanding.

Leisure

Fire's idea of leisure may be to work till exhausted and then to play until bored. Always burning with new ideas and goals; relaxation is difficult. May use leisure as downtime to recharge batteries in preparation for the next task.

Order

Fire tends to have many projects going at once and usually organizes in the head rather than in neat files. Likes things functional and uncomplicated but may not be overly concerned about details.

Relationships

Fire is results driven and tends to relate on a "transactional" basis. Relationships may be tied to contributions and perceived value, even among friends and family. Tends to view others as less competent and "supervises" relationships.

Stress

Fire has a high tolerance for stress and handles extreme pressure as a fact of life. Frequently expresses frustration and anger at loss of control and then resolves the problem. Is said not to suffer from ulcers personally but may be a "carrier" because of bringing stress to others.

Success

Fire views success in terms of beating the odds, exceeding expectations, and acquiring power, prestige, and financial freedom. Is an early adopter of innovative, power-enhancing products. Tends to be entrepreneurial and values independence rather than depending on others.

Tasks

Fire emphasizes "doing" over "talking," so prefers starting projects quickly and enthusiastically but can be distracted by new tasks that demand pioneering vision—leaving team members without input or direction. Has difficulty completing tasks before beginning others. Does not enjoy extensive work with details.

SELF-COACHING TIPS

If you are an *Earth*, know that your tendency toward analysis may cause "project paralysis." Open up and receive new ideas. You are the element most capable of transforming thoughts into reality. Trust your capacity to handle change.

If you are a *Water*, know that your tendency to seek the path of least resistance may cause you to seek lower ground, when higher thought and harder actions may be necessary.

If you are a *Wind*, know that your active intellect is easily distracted by anything that moves. In order to achieve and maintain maximum power, keep your focus long enough to see the project through to completion.

If you are a *Fire*, know that you can easily be misled by the false fuel of flattery and a hunger for power.

○ ○ ○

In this chapter you have been presented with the basic "alphabet" of the four elements as they relate to personality. What may appear on the page as mere strings of words are in actuality the necessary foundation for moving forward in your understanding.

Once you get the basics down, like a child who has learned the alphabet, you will begin to "read" people and situations with ever-increasing levels of mastery.

THE ELEMENTS
IN THE REAL WORLD

The management of knowledge workers is a "marketing job."
And in marketing one does not begin with a question: "what do
we want?" One begins with the questions: "What does the other
party want?" "What are its values? What are its goals? What
does it consider results?"

—PETER R. DRUCKER[1]

Now let's see how these elements play out in real-world, interpersonal dynamics. Once you become familiar with the four elements of personality, you will begin to see them demonstrated every day, all around you.

Just this week, for example, I came across two newspaper articles that demonstrated distinct personality types on the same Olympic team.

A revealing article by Norm Frauenheim in the August 21, 2004, issue of the *Arizona Republic* profiled swimmer Gary Hall Jr. after his gold-medal winning swim. The article, titled "Defiant Triumph," went on to describe Hall's grabbing gold in the 50-meter Olympic freestyle. After you read the following few paragraphs, tell me which of the four elements—Earth, Water, Wind, or Fire— swimmer Gary Hall Jr. probably is:

The colors were red, white and blue. Gary Hall Jr. wore them as only he can. Bold, brash, and gold. Hall continues to swim against the tides in the fast fashion that always seems to land him in hot water—and at the top of the Olympic medal stand. "Defiance," he said.

That was his method, and his motivation . . .

His victory capped a crazy few days full of controversy over whether he should have been included in the 400 meter freestyle relay. He wasn't among the relay's final four Sunday for any number of reasons. But in the end, every reason works. They were the fuel, the dynamic mix, that propelled Hall to his fifth gold medal in three Olympics. (Section A, page 1)

I was not surprised when the following day another article appeared that said Hall had been fined $5,000 for wrapping himself up in a version of the American flag that he had designed. Based on the events related in this article, Gary Hall Jr. displays all of the characteristics of Fire at its most intense—stirring up controversy, creating hot water, being nicknamed "Captain Defiance," and making sure that he got extra attention on the podium by designing his own flag. The fact that "for reasons unknown" he was not asked to swim on the relay team may also demonstrate Fire's natural tendency to seek the glory and not make the needs of a team a priority.

Contrast his Fire personality type with that of teammate Michael Phelps. His headline read, "Gracious Phelps Takes 5th; Hands Spot on Relay to Hard Luck Crocker." Also by Norm Frauenheim of the *Arizona Republic*, August 21, 2004, the report detailed how Phelps, in line for yet another gold medal, decided instead to hand his chance to swim in the final of the medley relay to his teammate Ian Crocker. Crocker, his archrival whom he had beaten for the gold in the 100-meter butterfly, had been beset by flulike symptoms throughout the Olympic competition. Phelps graciously gave Crocker the chance to swim in his place, assuring Crocker of his own opportunity for a gold medal.

Phelps said, "I just wanted Ian to have another chance. We came in as a team, and we are going home as a team." In this particular instance, Phelps displayed the sensitivities and non-ego bias of a Water personality type. Both swimmers were Olympic champions, yet their elemental personality styles made them winners in different ways.

CASE STUDY:
ELEMENTS ACTING IN HASTE LEADS TO POOR DECISION MAKING

When hiring decisions are made, it is often the flashy Fires who get the attention. In the book *The Daily Drucker* (HarperBusines, 2004), management guru Peter F. Drucker recalls a heated debate about hiring that took place one time in the General Motors executive committee. It seemed that the whole committee was in agreement on one candidate. This person had handled this crisis superbly, solved that problem beautifully, quenched yonder fire with great aplomb, etc. Suddenly the CEO, Mr. Sloan, broke in.

"A very impressive record your Mr. Smith has," he said, "but do explain to me how he gets into all those crises he then so brilliantly surmounts?" Nothing more was heard of Mr. Smith. When evaluating another candidate, Mr. Sloan said . . . "you know all the things you say that Mr. George cannot do? How come he got as far as he did? What *can* he do?" And when Mr. Sloan was told, he would say "Alright, he's not brilliant, and not fast, and looks drab, perhaps, but hasn't he always *performed?*" And Mr. George turned into one of the most successful general managers in a big division at a difficult time.

Mr. Sloan aptly recognized that Fire people have a tendency to create the very crises they then can claim to solve. In this particular instance, Sloan dug deeper and found a less flashy, but more solid, Earth candidate that turned out to be the best fit.

USING THE ELEMENTS TO HANDLE "INFLAMED" CUSTOMERS

In a training seminar we did with Wal-Mart, one of the associates laughed and said, "You wouldn't believe what happened the other day. A customer came in and started complaining very loudly to me. He was starting to get madder and madder, and at one point he actually reached out and shoved me. Knowing that I am a Fire, I quickly grabbed Alicia, who is a Water, and literally put her between me and the customer so I wouldn't go off on him before we got the situation resolved."

I told him that was very wise, but then asked, "What would you have done if Alicia had not been nearby?"

He said, "I would have asked myself, 'Now how would Alicia handle this?'" and everybody laughed.

Knowing what your element is, and isn't, is a valuable coaching tool that can be used when your missing element is most in need.

WHEN TWO ELEMENTS GET TOGETHER

My agent Terry Barber and I love to get together. With our mutual travel schedules, it is often easy to meet in airports, even when we are flying in different directions.

Twice when we have met, we have gotten so caught up in talking about everything that we have completely missed our flights. Both of us are Wind/Fires, and we get so excited about new ideas and opportunities that we sometimes miss the realities of the simple steps in front of us. So now when we get together, one of us says, "Okay, one of us needs to be Earth here. Let's pull out our itineraries, write down what time we need to be where, and make sure we get to our gates on time."

WHEN YOUR ELEMENT IS MISUNDERSTOOD

Once I began to see how the elements affect our lives, our thinking, and our teamwork, I heard stories every day about how knowledge of these facts could make a difference.

For example, one of my friends is a highly respected consultant who earns in the high six figures. Let's call him "Bill." Bill signed on as an associate with his friend "Sam" to help him build his consulting firm. Bill is very good at what he does, and he takes his work seriously. He shared with me that he was devastated a month earlier when "Amy," one of the principals of the company, took him aside and said angrily, "Bill, I think you are lazy." Bill was shocked to hear this. He asked her why she felt that way. She said, "Because you breeze in and out of the office any time you feel like it. Half the time you are not at your desk, and the other half of the time nobody knows where you are. We never see you around here, and it is pulling the rest of us down because we are working our hearts out for the team, and you should be too."

Bill said he had to count to ten under his breath before he responded. "Amy," he began, "how many of your daughter's soccer games have you missed this year?"

"One," she responded.

Bill said, "I have made only one out of twenty-six of my son's games because I have been out on the road drumming up business. How many red-eye flights at 1:00 a.m. have you taken cross-country this year?"

"None," she admitted.

"How many Saturday night stays have you booked at look-alike hotel rooms so you could save the firm money by staying over the weekend?"

"None," she admitted again.

By that time, Bill was on a roll. "I have logged more than two hundred thousand miles this year alone meeting with clients from one coast to the other. I have helped secure clients that this firm never even knew existed, and I have done it by being in front of them, face-to-face, and asking them who their friends were, and then meeting with them face-to-face. My contacts have increased this firm's billing by 25 percent in the last quarter alone. My desk is not really next to yours and Sam's—it is in seat 25B on Delta Air Lines. So if I seem to breeze in and out of the office when I feel like it, pausing just long enough to get my files or drop some old ones off, just know that I am contributing to the team the very best way I know how. Even when you can't see it."

After Bill shared this with me, his head dropped to his chest, and he looked away. "I'm thinking of resigning," he said. "I cannot believe that they feel I am not contributing to the team. I don't want to work with people who can be so blind to what I am doing."

Bill's resignation from this fledgling firm would cost it easily one-quarter of its current billings and untold amounts of possible referral business from that core. He is a highly paid professional, working with highly paid professionals, yet because he does not feel seen or valued, he is thinking of leaving the firm.

What element would you guess Amy is? What element do you think Bill is? If you guessed Earth and Wind, respectively, you would be right.

As I shared with Bill my thoughts on his element, he burst out laughing. "Yes, I am a Wind, I guess. I even deliberately mow my lawn in a zigzag pattern just to drive my next-door neighbor crazy. I change the mowing pattern every week, and he can hardly contain himself. He must be an Earth!"

Bill howled in delight at this realization about himself and his neighbor. Whether this knowledge will allow him to remain in his position at the consulting firm currently remains to be seen.

Case Study: Persuading Someone to Accept a New Idea

I was a speaker at a convent in Illinois. One of the young nuns approached me at the break and said, "Laurie Beth, you have to help us!" Not knowing how I could possibly help, but wanting to, I asked Sister Marie what the problem was. She replied, "I have been trying for six months to get Mother Superior to sign off on this purchase order for a new computer system for the school. I have told her that if we don't make some radical changes, this school is going to become outdated and possibly go under. Yet she insists that we write out everything by hand and do things as we have done them for the last fifty years. She says, 'This way has worked for the convent for the last fifty years, and there is certainly no reason to change things now!'"

Based on our initial discussion of the elements, I asked Sister Marie which elements she believed Mother Superior to be. "Oh definitely an Earth!" she replied.

"Okay. I'd like you to go into the next room for fifteen minutes and study the list of Earth words we wrote down as a group. Then come back and, in front of

"I EVEN DELIBERATELY MOW MY LAWN IN A ZIGZAG PATTERN JUST TO DRIVE MY NEXT-DOOR NEIGHBOR CRAZY. I CHANGE THE MOWING PATTERN EVERY WEEK, AND HE CAN HARDLY CONTAIN HIMSELF. HE MUST BE AN EARTH!"—BILL

everyone, make your pitch for the computer system again, but this time use 85 percent Earth words in your appeal.

The young nun did as suggested, and when she returned, her appeal sounded like this: "Mother Superior, this school has been around for more than one hundred years. Our roots go so deeply into the community soil that almost every current leader can claim to have graduated from this firm foundation."

Mother Superior was nodding approvingly as Sister Marie continued:

"However, there is a real and growing threat to our longevity."

"What is it, child?" asked the suddenly alarmed Mother.

"Our roots are withering and dying because of a lack of the proper nutrients. And unless we provide the proper care and feeding to this broken system soon, all that we have worked for may dry up and fade away."

By this time Mother Superior was very alarmed.

"Tell me what we need to do!"

"We need to computerize the school," the young nun said quietly.

"Why haven't you told me this before?" asked the Mother, who reached for the proposal and signed it with a firm signature.

In this case, the young nun did not change her request, but used her new knowledge of her boss's Earth-like values to place the appeal in a more favorable light. Your knowledge of the elements can help you do the same.

UNDERSTANDING ELEMENTS IN COUPLES

There is no team unit more precious, or obviously difficult to maintain, than that of *couples*.

A couple shared with me how they were using their new knowledge of the elements. Dan is a Wind/Fire, and his wife, Julie, is a Fire/Earth. They have started a business together that allows them to use his gifts as a consultant with hers as an educator. As anyone knows who has worked in a family business, things can get hot at times.

When you have two Fires working together, things can get really hot. One day tempers began to flare, and Julie said, "Dan, I know exactly what we need. Let's not say another word." He quieted down and let her drive them to a place in the city that has a huge fountain in the middle of a lake. "Let's just sit here and take in this setting for twenty minutes, and then we can talk," she said. As they sat by the lake and the fountain, the beauty and serenity of the water began to work on their attitudes. Perhaps it was not just the water setting that helped, but it was also the "Waterlike" action of taking time for contemplation and quiet reflection that helped put things in perspective and calm things down between them.

Julie is so sold on the value of the elements in her understanding of self that now she disciplines herself to allow time for a long, soaking bath every night. Whereas before she often worked late into the evening, always aware of what else could be done, she now makes sure she gets plenty of "in the water" time, and she is sleeping better for it. Fire / Earth combinations tend toward workaholism, so adding plenty of the reflection time of Water and the spontaneity and fun of Wind can help bring inner balance and harmony.

Meanwhile, Dan, a Wind/Fire combination, is helping to balance himself by swimming daily and taking long walks in nature. He travels quite a bit, and he says, "Now when I get home, I literally go and touch the grass for a few moments, just to help ground myself and my thinking."

Later in the book I will provide more stories for you on which you can practice your diagnostic skills. Now, however, let's consider some anger styles of the elements.

ANGER STYLES

Conflict and anger are parts of life, and the more differences between individuals, the more likely conflict is to occur. Therefore, if you know the innate anger style and tendency of the elemental makeup of the person you are dealing with, the more likely you are to diffuse and/or survive the anger.

The anger styles I talk about are those of the raw, immature element. The hope is that as we mature, we learn to modify and control these natural tendencies. Here are summaries of these styles:

- *Fire*: hot, intense, explosive, dangerous, out of control. Duration: usually brief, short episodes.

- *Wind*: sudden, intense, noisy, throwing things, howling. Duration: usually brief, short episodes, seldom holds grudges, and often forgets what the fuss was about.

- *Water*: slow simmer, boils, scalds, evaporates and disappears, or gathers its friends and floods. Duration: slow to boil but rarely returns in the same form once it evaporates. Floods are rare but can be devastating.

- *Earth*: buries its anger, masks its emotions, holds grudges. Duration: very slow, can take years to build. Severe consequences when it does erupt (as a volcano) or quake (along "fault" lines).

Earth's Anger Style

When I ask people in my seminar, "Could an Earth person be angry at you and you not know it?" the immediate answer called out by the group is "Yes!" When I ask, "How long could an Earth person be angry at you and you not know it?" they call out even louder, "Forever!"

The tendency of Earth is to bury its anger. Indeed, you could go years and not be aware of how much anger Earth contains until suddenly, and often without warning, the Earth quakes, and your whole world is turned upside down. Earth is not confrontational by nature. It assumes that it can handle anything that comes its way and finds a place for it somehow. Earth will survive, no matter what, and since it isn't given to drama, it will try to keep things "grounded" and in order.

I have an acquaintance who is an Earth person. She married about four years ago, and she has been gaining a lot of weight ever since. When we all go to dinner, this friend hardly talks. Her husband does all the talking and decision making, and he boasts about how happy they are together.

But when I look at her, I wonder. If she is so happy, why is she literally stuffing her emotions? That is another anger style of Earth, and it can be deadly in the long run, even if the short-term result seems to be peace.

The way to avoid having an earthquake or an overstuffed Earth person as a friend is to check in constantly, even being so bold as to ask, "Is there anything I have said or done in the last fifteen minutes that upsets you?" Then, give an Earth time to speak—lots of time. And wait for the answer. You'll be glad you did.

It also would help to reread the likes and dislikes of Earths, and adapt your words and actions accordingly, whenever and wherever possible. Learning what they need and like shows respect, and respect is the foundation for any solid relationship.

Water's Anger Style

When water gets hot, it boils, steams, scalds, and then disappears. Water can also be given to flooding, but usually heavy rains fall first as a warning. If things get too cold, water turns to ice. Thin ice—as in "you are skating on it." I'm sure you can relate to or have experienced these anger styles if you are involved with a Water person.

On a plane not long ago the man sitting beside me began to talk about his divorce. He said, "I don't know what happened with Sally. I thought we were happy. Then one day she up and took the kids and was gone."

I asked him how many kids they had, and he said, "Six." I asked what ages they were, and he said, "Three to fourteen." I asked him what he did for a living, and he said, "I travel a lot." I asked him if he had ever noticed his wife crying in the kitchen, and he said, "Yes, but I thought it was just because she's always so sentimental."

That man was not aware of his wife's needs or hurts, didn't check in, didn't offer to relieve her with the kids, and despite her many warnings, via tears, of her unhappiness, he was shocked when she "suddenly" evaporated. My question is, how long did he leave the water on the fire before it disappeared? If she was a Water and he was a Wind, what elements were probably needed but missing in their lives, especially with six kids on the scene?

Another anger style of Water is ice. I've seen many unhappy Waters turn to ice, which brings to mind the term *frigid conditions*. Believe me, there is probably some anger or things wouldn't be so frosty. Ice on sidewalks is almost as treacherous as ice on the roads, a fact I learned one winter in Toledo, Ohio. An acquaintance slipped and fell on his back while he was getting into his car and nearly froze to death before help arrived an hour later. Little patches of ice in a home setting—how deadly can that be?

The best way to deal with boiling Water in anger is to turn down the heat or do your best to remove the source of its frustration. Don't lean too far over the pot. Look at what's underneath, and you'll do well to cool things down.

As for Water in ice anger situations, obviously the thing to do is to try to warm things up. Communicate. Ask about feelings. Water is the most sensitive of all the elements and absorbs things from all around its environment. You might not even be to blame.

A friend who is a Water admitted that she burst into tears one time because she drove by a warehouse that had been abandoned. Her husband, who is a sensitive Earth guy, asked her gently what was wrong, and she cried, "Look at the beautiful building that nobody wants anymore." This led to a discussion on commitment and taking care of things that you love, and she was fine by the time they got home. It is interesting to me that the term *husband* means "gardener," which implies a lot of earth tending and watering of the wife. Good image. I like it.

Wind's Anger Style

The anger style of Wind is to howl, whine, or suddenly toss things up into the air for no seeming reason. The image from the movie *Twister* of a cow coming at a car in the middle of a tornado is a good one for Wind. You might be going along thinking everything is fine, when suddenly a twister appears on the horizon, and before you know it, you are getting everything you've ever done and the kitchen sink thrown at you. Most of it is for effect, and it seldom lasts long, so the best thing to do with an angry Wind is to let it howl and get out of its way.

If you want the whining to stop, however, you need to attend to that creaky gate or broken shutter that you've been meaning to fix, but haven't. Winds like to yell, they love to see things in motion, they want something moved because they were there, and it doesn't really matter much what. So, another strategy for dealing with a Wind in anger is to lie low till it blows over or get up and move something around until the howling stops. Fix something.

THE IMAGE FROM THE MOVIE *TWISTER* OF A COW COMING AT A CAR IN THE MIDDLE OF A TORNADO IS A GOOD ONE FOR WIND.

Take a drive together. Rearrange the pictures on the wall. Rearrange your schedule to make more time for this Wind. Remove obstacles to his or

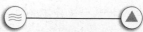

her free expression. Agree to take that trip. Just let the Wind know that he or she is being seen and heard and understood, and things should calm down.

Fire's Anger Style

Fire's anger style is to flare, jump, and rage. Fire, like Wind, is given to drama. Also like Wind, its anger is usually short-lived, though intense. It is not unusual for a Fire to come home from work, walk in the door, and have a temper fit because somebody left the bike in the driveway. Fire then proceeds to tell the family members how lazy and inconsiderate they are, and they ought to be more like him (the Fire). After a few minutes of this, the Fire person usually calms down, looks around at the frightened family hunkered around, and then says, "There, I feel much better now. What say we all go out and get a pizza?" Meanwhile, the Earth teenage son says not a word but silently thinks, *I will not talk to you until I graduate, if I do, which I might not, just to get back at you.* The Wind daughter says, "Wow, Dad, you sure were hot! Okay, let's go. I'm hungry!" The wife, who is a Water, creates chilly conditions in the bedroom that night.

Does any of this sound familiar?

Once, a disc jockey was to interview me on a radio show. As we sat down and adjusted the microphones, he said, "I just had a fight with my ex-wife, and I'm telling you I am so hot, I'm not sure I can even think straight." Realizing that this was to be an hour-long talk show, I was somewhat dismayed. Quickly I decided to put the four elements program into action. I told him about the four elements, and we did a quick assessment of what each was and did. I asked him which element he most related to, and he said, "Fire!"

I then asked him how Fire might handle the situation with his ex-wife, whatever that situation might be. He got quiet for a moment and then said, "I could blast through there in a righteous rage and leave everything in ashes. Or I could surround the situation with warmth and light, and wait for the truth to emerge." He took a deep breath, looked at me, and said, "Thank you. I know now what I must do." And the show continued with him in a much calmer frame of mind.

WHAT'S YOUR ANGER STYLE?

Once you recognize your natural anger style, you can control and modify it before "instinct" takes over and you merely react. I went horseback riding with a friend who is a Fire. He hadn't ridden in some time, and I offered him a gentler horse from the stable, but being a Fire and loving drama and attention, he opted to ride my new, relatively unbroken Arabian stallion.

We headed into the fields with my two dogs running alongside when suddenly a rabbit jumped out from the alfalfa and took off running with the dogs in hot pursuit. The stallion quite predictably spooked, reared up, and ran with its tail in the air, heading straight for a ditch, which it thankfully and narrowly jumped. At long last the horse finally came to a trembling halt, and I galloped up beside them to see if they were okay.

My Fire friend was in a rage. Within seconds he blasted me and my dogs and my crazy horse and this crazy field with crooked ditches and . . . and . . . and . . .

My natural tendency as a Wind, in a high adrenaline situation, was to jump into it with him. I wanted to yell at him for being so vain as to take an unbroken horse and put my dogs and my stallion and the ditch and the rabbit at risk as well. However, I caught myself. *You're a Wind, Laurie, remember, and he's a Fire. What is best to do here?* So I caught my breath and literally backed up my horse until I was not next to him, but about five feet away while he continued to rant and rave.

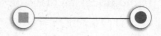

After about two minutes of this, he sputtered to a halt in his words. He looked at me and at the dogs, who had returned without the rabbit, and at his saddle, which was askew, and he started to laugh. Then I started to laugh, and we began to howl together about how ridiculous and funny the situation was. We straightened his saddle and spent the rest of the day happy and exhilarated by our mutual adventure.

JUST BECAUSE YOU HAVE A NATURAL TENDENCY TO BE A CERTAIN ELEMENT . . . DOES NOT GIVE YOU THE EXCUSE TO ABUSE THAT TENDENCY OR ACT OUT ITS "RAWNESS" AND EXPECT OTHER PEOPLE TO ADAPT.

What would have happened if I hadn't caught myself and controlled my natural elemental tendency? One of us would have been walking home—and I wouldn't have been the one doing the walking.

A word here. Just because you have a natural tendency to be a certain element or behave like a certain element does not give you the excuse to abuse that tendency or act out its "rawness" and expect other people to adapt.

Of course, you *can* do that, and people do it all the time, which is perhaps why our divorce rate is so high and why our teenage runaway problem is epidemic and people get fired or demoted or imprisoned. All of it "natural"?

GETTING RESULTS USING THE ELEMENTS

Now let's see how to use your knowledge of the elements to your advantage. Following are case studies of how people used their new-found understandings of the different elemental needs and desires in order to gain peace and resolution in the situation. Answering the discussion questions, either by yourself or in a group, will help deepen your understanding of the elements.

Case Study: When Mom Can't Stay Home

Lisa is a high-powered sales executive who thrives on challenge. She does so well in her job that her husband, Bob, has chosen to stay home and help raise their two boys, who are eight and ten years old. Because Lisa works in the telecommunications industry, she is given many options for career advancement, almost all of which involve relocation.

The constant moves were causing strain on the marriage and home life. When Lisa and her husband arrived at a Path seminar, things had gotten so tense between them that they were barely speaking. She wanted to take the next career advancement offer, which would involve a move of more than a thousand miles, and he wanted to stay put.

It didn't take long for the two of them to grasp their natural elements. Lisa, as you probably guessed, is a Wind, and her nurturing, root-conscious husband is an Earth. Suddenly many of their life differences became clear.

That next week I received an e-mail from Lisa stating that her husband and the two boys had offered her a proposal. They presented it to her like this:

"Mom, we want to stay put for a while. We want to have the

same set of friends and know who our teachers are going to be and not have to move around so much. If you will agree to commit to stay in this town for the next three years, we *promise* to help you rearrange the furniture at least once a week and take trips every other weekend."

Lisa said she looked at their proposal and accepted it. "I can live with that," she said. After she signed it, the boys and her husband went outside and literally hugged the tree in their front yard.

Food for Thought

- Why were Lisa and her husband, Bob, different in their approach to life? How did realizing their elements help solve the conflict?

- What did her husband and sons wisely offer in exchange for her turning down the move?

- Why would this offer have some appeal for a Wind?

- Where in your life is there a conflict that might be due to different elements trying to get their needs met?

- What possible compromise could each element offer the other one without making anyone "wrong" for what each wants?

Case Study: Would This Be a Good Match?

After John received his law degree, he got a secure job with a leading law firm in town. Now he is ready to settle down. He has already purchased a home and has money saved in the bank. He is currently dating Sheila, a redhead who has informed him that she plans to go to Europe, race cars, and run for political office. He is crazy about her, wants to marry her, but insists that she give up her plans for travel and school. She is extremely attracted to him, especially the security he offers, but is torn. What should she do?

Food for Thought
- John is probably a ___earth___ .
- Sheila is probably a ___wind___ .

- Discuss why they would or would not make a good match, and what they would need to recognize in order for the marriage to work.

Case Study: How to Get Your Patio Built in Three Days or Less

I always test my material on my friends and family. After I had shared the PEP idea with a close friend whom I shall call "Paula," she decided to try an experiment.

"Paula" is an Earth, and her husband, "Dan" is a Wind. She had been trying to get him to build their patio for approximately three years. She was approaching the situation like this: "Dan, when are you going to build the patio?" But this approach was bearing no fruit since all she had in their unfinished backyard was dirt.

After Paula studied the characteristics of elements and was quite sure that she had the proper fit for her husband, she came up with a plan. She shared it with me laughingly over lunch three weeks later.

She said, "Laurie, you're not going to believe what happened. Thinking about Dan as being a Wind, I decided to try this. One Saturday morning I woke up and said, 'Honey, let's just get in the truck and go for a drive today doing anything we want! I'll cancel my hair appointment, and we can just go!'" She said he leaped out of bed and put his boots on so fast, it almost made her head spin.

They got into the truck and started driving, stopping at all his favorite places. After lunch she said, "Let's just take a turn here and stop in at Home Depot for a minute, okay?" He said, "Sure," and they wandered over to the garden section. Paula said, "Look, Honey, bricks are on sale! Let's get some and toss them into the back of the truck while we're here." Dan agreed, and at least Paula had her bricks in the truck. Still, an assembled patio was a long way off.

As they were driving back to their home, she said, "I've been thinking. What if we invited all our friends over this weekend and had them write their names on bricks, and then they could help us install them? We could order some barbecue ribs from Chris's and make it a party!" Dan loved the idea and promptly got on his cell phone and began inviting friends over.

That weekend they had fifty friends on their hands and knees laughingly and happily installing bricks in the sunburst pattern that Paula had designed. By midnight, she had her patio, and it had taken only three days.

Food for Thought

- Why was Paula's first approach with Dan not working?
- What words does a Wind *not* like to hear that she was using?
- Why did her new approach work so fast and so well?
- What did she do differently as a result of the knowledge of Dan's element?
- What parts of her strategy were appealing to a Wind?
- Do you have a project that is stalled? How have you been approaching the key "elements" that need to help you get it done?

How Young Can You Know?

While conducting a seminar in Tucson for a leadership team, I heard one woman gasp and say, "Now I get it!" She raised her hand and said, "Excuse me for interrupting, but I just have to share this. I have a four-year-old son who wakes up every morning, gets out every last one of his toys, scatters them around the room, and then proceeds to run in circles until he makes himself dizzy. And I have been so frustrated, following along behind him, restacking the toys and telling him to put things away. Now I realize that he is a Wind, and I am an Earth. His job is to scatter!" The whole group burst into laughter.

When I was sharing the story about the little boy getting out all his toys and running around in circles until he made himself dizzy, my friend Terry Barber chuckled and said, "Laurie Beth, that is exactly the way I work!"

All joking aside, imagine the value of what the mother gained in learning the differences between her and her son. This conceivably could alleviate or even prevent a lifetime of frustration as she learns to recognize and deal with his hard wiring.

Some might say, "Aren't all children like the wind?" In my experience, the answer is no. I remember my friend's five-year-old son wanting to carefully stack everything in his mother's grocery cart in order. As he got older, say, six or seven, he used to follow her around with the list and take items out as she put them in, saying, "You don't need that. I don't see it written down here." When he was nine, he informed his parents one day that they didn't need to buy health insurance for him because he had learned that if they took him to the emergency ward at the downtown clinic, everything would be free. I am proud to say he is an attorney today, putting his list-making and organizational skills to good use, as well as his awareness of the rights of all citizens.

Case Study: Should Maria Switch Schools?

Maria had been a schoolteacher for more than twenty-five years. She taught art to seventh graders and loved it. However, the school had a new principal who was driving all of the other teachers crazy. The principal was so focused on getting the school achievement test scores up that she was draining the joy out of the process for the teachers. She spoke in military tones, issued ultimatums, set strict deadlines, and always seemed to be asking more and more from the teachers who were already burning the midnight oil. Six teachers had already transferred, and the fifteen who remained had approached Maria and asked her to be an intermediary between them and the principal.

Maria had gotten so nervous about the pressure from the principal that she had begun to break out in hives. She was losing sleep at night, and she dreaded going to school for the first time in all those years of teaching.

The principal had a reputation in the district as being a hard-nosed, uncompromising, and rather caustic person. Maria's dilemma was that she didn't want to let her teacher friends down, but she wasn't sure she wanted to be the spokesperson for the group either. Her question to our group was: "Should I resign early, transfer, or do what the other teachers are asking?"

Food for Thought

- Based on what you know, which element would you guess Maria is?

- Which element would you guess the principal is?

- Regardless of what element she is, what element were the other teachers asking Maria to become?

- If you discerned that Maria was a Water, how did you arrive at that?

- Why might a Water be more sensitive to a caustic situation than others?

- If Maria stays in that job, what might be the cost to her?

- Since Maria is a Water, why was she so afraid to let the others down?

- What do you think it would take for Maria to decide to become the spokesperson they are seeking?

- Is there a situation in your life that might be causing you anxiety because you feel responsible to other people?

- If so, what does your PEP assessment say your strengths and weaknesses are in this regard?

Case Study: Can Fred Win Angie's Heart?

Fred, a very successful traveling salesman, is crazy about Angie. He has asked her to marry him on three different occasions—once, right out of high school. Angie, recovering from a ten-year marriage and divorce, is hesitant to jump into anything too soon.

She wants to see her daughter go to college before she moves anyone new into the house. Fred sends Angie cards and flowers nearly once a week. He ships exotic gifts to her from trips that he takes around the world. He calls her constantly. He drops in and surprises her at work, a job that she has held for fifteen years.

Fred insists that the love in his heart will never die, even though he has had three short-term relationships in the past and has no long-term contract with the company that hired him twelve months ago. Angie admits that her heart leaps whenever Fred appears on the scene, but she is frightened. Fred, unable to take yet another rejection, turns on his heels and heads straight to the airport in retreat.

Food for Thought

- Fred is probably a _____.

- Angie is probably a _____.

- Name three things Fred could do to speak to Angie's heart in ways that she probably values.

Case Study: Father and Daughter

Amelia has always been creative. After fifteen years as a teacher, she moved to Santa Fe to pursue her dream of being a professional artist. She began to thrive in the atmosphere of physical beauty and diversity, and she asked her father, Jim, to visit her.

Her father was a farmer from the heartland of America and had never really understood his free-spirited daughter, which had caused quite a bit of friction in their relationship. However, he did come to see her in the city. As they were sitting on the patio, she remarked how much she loved the area and the different cultures that were represented.

Jim mumbled, "They are all just a bunch of hippies if you ask me. Why on earth would anybody in her right mind want to live here?"

Amelia began to cry, trying to defend through her tears the people she had grown to love, saying, "They are not hippies; they are artists."

Unhappy that he had once again upset his daughter, Jim promptly got up, walked to his truck, and left.

Two hours later he came back with a pear tree in his truck. Without a word he got out, dug a hole, and planted it in Amelia's garden. He looked up at her, tipped his hat, dusted off his blue jeans, and then left.

Food for Thought

- Which element is Amelia? Why?

- Which element is Jim? Why?

- How did Jim express his affection for his daughter without using words?

- What was his medium of choice?

- Why did he and Amelia probably view "hippies" differently?

SECTION SUMMARY

This section provided an overview of how different elements react and act in various work and life scenarios. My intention (and hope) from the case studies and stories presented here is that you will begin to truly see the elementary personality differences as causes of—and solutions to—conflict and begin to use your understanding to apply wisdom to situations that might have seemed "unsolvable" before.

In the next section we further explore how to apply your new knowledge.

PART II

Applying the Elements

3

UNDERSTANDING TEAM DYNAMICS: PUTTING IT ALL TOGETHER

"Any organization develops people; it either forms them or deforms them."

—PETER F. DRUCKER[1]

They charged into the meeting, incensed because of an e-mail that had gone out that morning.

Person B, who had received the e-mail from Person A, stood up and said, "I can't work under these conditions. All I have to say to you, A, is, 'Lead, follow, or get out of the way!'"

Person A said, "That's funny. I was going to say exactly the same thing to you!"

Person C pulled out the agenda and said, "Let's get going. We are already behind schedule. As you can see on page thirty-four of this report . . ."

Person D interrupted and said, "Let's review the notes from our last meeting first. I think you can see, A, that a lot of groundwork has already been done."

Person E said, "C, if you get out those spreadsheets and begin to plow *through them right now, I am going to pull out a gun and shoot myself." (E was kidding, of course, but it was enough to change the atmosphere.) E said, "Can't you see that everyone is upset? We need to take time and express what we're really feeling."*

Person D leaned over and whispered to Person A, "Right now I am just trying to hold this team together. B is ready to walk."

Person A looked at the clock. It was 9:45 a.m. on a Monday. The week had just begun.

If this scenario feels familiar, you are already aware of the world of team dynamics. In this not-so-fictional scenario, every one of those individuals was a highly professional, highly paid, and deeply committed person. Perhaps with your reading of the book so far you can quickly pinpoint the elements in their personalities that were at play (or war). Not one person in that room was bad, mean, or stupid, yet unless and until the team dynamic came together, everything on the table was going nowhere.

In the following pages we will increase your intuitive understanding of how to work with the elements to make them more productive as individuals and as a team. I will first give an overview of team make-ups with possible consequences and then show how people view themselves as elements within a team.

THE CHEMISTRY OF TEAMWORK

Reports and numbers are really just little black marks on paper. The people surrounding them, with that indefinable essence of chemistry and commitment that we call teamwork, make things happen—or not.

Knowing the elementary makeup of your team, as well as their mission and vision statements, can help you get alignment with the various duties and challenges that arise.

For example, the administrators of a charter school that we work with in Phoenix, Arizona, told us that they had launched an impressive "Start Your Own Business" initiative for the seniors. "Every senior was to identify his or her business, build a Web site, and then market it in order to help raise funds for college. We even set up a matching fund for every dollar they earned," said the principal. An assessment later indicated that she is a Wind/Fire.

"How did it go?" I asked her, already anticipating the answer.

"It flopped. No one around here can figure out what went wrong either," she said.

Perhaps you figured out, as I did, that not every senior has the elementary makeup to want to launch and market a business. Typically Winds and Fires are going to be the natural entrepreneurs, while the Waters and Earths are not going to be drawn to that kind of high-energy, high-focused, unstructured "Wild West" activity.

IS YOUR TEAM TILTED TOWARD ONE ELEMENT?

Now that we have the capabilities of literally seeing the elemental makeup of team members through the PEP assessment, the results have been exciting in a number of ways. For example, I consulted with a billion-dollar organization, and the seventy-one executive team members took their profiles. What emerged was revealing (and was provided to them in a detailed team report). Essentially the CEO was working with a group of fifty-eight Fire/Earths, twelve Wind/Fires, and only one Water, which was him, the CEO.

Remembering that Fire/Earths are the ones who are results oriented and also tend toward workaholic perfectionism, I was not surprised at what happened after I presented the findings to the team. It seems they had hired a firm to do customer surveys, and the person who was in charge of the report described her findings immediately following my presentation. "Here is the summary of what we found," she began. "In a few sentences, it is this. Customers appreciate your results. However, they do not feel that you care about them as people. They stated that you don't listen well, and you don't take the time with them that they feel they deserve."

The CEO leaned over and whispered to me, "No wonder. Look at our team configuration." He was grasping a very important lesson in elemental team dynamics.

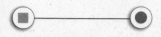

WHEN YOUR TEAM'S ELEMENTAL COMPOSITION IS TILTED TOWARD ONE OR TWO OF THE ELEMENTS, YOUR RESULTS ARE GOING TO SKEW IN THAT DIRECTION. SO, IF YOU HAVE A TEAM OF FIRE /EARTHS, THEY ARE GOING TO PRODUCE WHAT FIRES AND EARTHS MOST VALUE, WHICH IS RESULTS.

When your team's elemental composition is tilted toward one or two of the elements, your results are going to skew in that direction. So, if you have a team of Fire/Earths, they are going to produce what Fires and Earths most value, which is results. However, you are also going to produce that elemental combination's accompanying weakness or challenge, which is relationships. In this case, the CEO's Fire/Earth team was producing great results, but since team members were not naturally inclined toward, and thus did not greatly value, relationship skills, this vital (Water) customer concern was missing.

In another public company I worked with, the thirty-five-member executive team included mostly Earths and Waters, with Fires as the third most populated category. There were only three Winds on the entire team. The challenges of this organization were immense, not the least of which was public pressure because the company was in the headlines almost daily.

It seems the company was being accused of doing things the way things have always been done and failing to produce results that were in keeping with the times. The organization, rather than innovating, was heavily defending itself on its Web site against the claims. I had to wonder: perhaps if there were more Winds on the team, listening to customers and looking for new ways of approaching problems, this organization's ability to innovate and thus change would have been improved. As of this writing I have been actively engaged to help institute change throughout the entire organization. (If you don't have enough Winds on your team, hire some. There are always plenty hovering around, eager to bring in new ideas.)

In another seminar I created a scenario for Sally, a Wind: she had done a field survey and was to recommend that the company open a new office in Nevada. I asked her to speak to a committee made up of three Earths from the group and use her own language to convey her enthusiasm.

She said, "I've seen what is out there, and I'm telling you we need to move on this. If we don't act on this now, the competition is going to eat our lunch. I've located a couple of sites that show lots of possibility, and I told a realtor in the area that we would be putting in a bid on one of them this week."

The Earth committee members, all of whom had been standing with their arms folded across their chests, never cracked a smile or raised an eyebrow.

"What are the demographics out there? What is your plan?" asked one. "How in the world are we going to pay for that? Where will we get the people to sustain it?" asked another.

Sally took a step backward at each question, and you could literally see her energy going down. I asked her how she was feeling.

"I don't think they get it!" she explained in exasperation. "Why are they trying to make this so hard? Don't they trust what I am saying to them?"

Meanwhile, the Earth team was standing there, unmoving.

I turned to the audience and said, "Okay, now watch what happens. Earth, give her your response."

One of them said, "We are going to need a lot more paperwork before we even begin to consider this." Another one said, "If you'd like to submit a form to get on the budget agenda for next month's meeting, I can get you one. I have them in my desk downstairs." The third said, "I'm not sure we have the resources for this."

With that, Sally, discouraged, sat down.

I then turned to the Earth committee and asked them how they were feeling about her idea. "I thought it was great!" admitted one of them. "Me too," said another. "She showed a lot of passion. If she brought me more documentation, I'd be totally for it."

By that time the audience was beginning to snicker. It became apparent that the Earth team members were actually excited about it, but excitement never made it to their faces. Nor did their body lan-

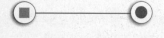

WHILE WINDS
VALUE CHANGE
AND EXCITEMENT,
AND ARE INDEED
USUALLY THE FIRST
ONES TO SENSE
OPPORTUNITIES,
THEY ARE OFTEN
"SHOT DOWN" BY
WELL-MEANING
BUT EARTH-TYPE
COMMITTEES.

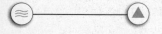

guage convey acceptance or enthusiasm.

"What do you want from us?" said one of them good-naturedly. "Our job is to guard the resources. We can't be flying off willy-nilly every time someone in marketing comes up with an idea."

The point was made. While Winds value change and excitement, and are indeed usually the first ones to sense opportunities, they are often "shot down" by well-meaning but Earth-type committees. Both elements have their parts to play, yet if Winds are not listened to, valued, or appreciated, they will die at their desks or leave for parts more promising. If the Winds leave an organization, the breath is literally taken out of it, and the organization will be stuck in the status quo. Likewise, if there are no Earths to balance a team, Winds can lead the organization in all sorts of directions, sometimes simultaneously, which will not produce favorable results.

Synergy: a Result of Understanding the Makeup of Your Team

Imagine that you have a team of Fires and Waters. This group would constantly get fired up only to put itself out. Earth/Water teams could be fertile, but could end up just being mud. All Fire teams burn themselves out. Wind/Earth teams mostly stir up dust. You get the point. A team leader must understand the elementary makeup of the team and balance it accordingly.

In Seattle I worked with three siblings in a family-owned business. The older brother was the CEO, the sister was the front desk customer service person, and the younger brother was in sales and marketing.

Brother Joe, the CEO, took me aside and told me he was having problems because customers were leaving in droves since his sister took over customer service, and sales were dropping because his brother couldn't seem to close a sale. Jill, the sister, was often seem slamming down the phone in frustration, saying "What do you mean you need that phone number again? I gave it to you last week!" Jason, the brother, was often heard asking about the clients' families, friends, and vacation plans, but never closing in for the sale.

After we assessed the elementary makeup of the team, it became apparent that the sister was a Wind/Fire and the younger brother was a Water. The older brother, an Earth, was trying to maintain a sense of order, but the status quo was not working. Just because the sister was a woman didn't mean she would automatically offer the best "first impression" at the front desk, and just because the younger brother was a man didn't mean he was automatically good at sales.

When the Wind/Fire sister was switched into sales and marketing, and the Water brother was switched to customer service, sales improved dramatically.

An Elemental Exercise for Your Team

One of the biggest challenges facing all of the elements is understanding how to value and communicate with one another. A fun and educational exercise we do regarding the elements and teams comes from my friend Lee Ellis. We divide the room into four components. Those who feel they most "gravitate" to the element of Earth, for example, go toward corner one. Opposite them we place those who are most attracted to Wind. Catty-corner to them are the elements of Fire and Water, each in their own corner.

Then they are to convince me, the neutral party, that their element is "The Most Awesome Element." I ask them to list at least five to seven reasons. The groups leap into the task, and it is fun to watch their personalities evolve as the task proceeds.

In a seminar I did with the leadership team of a government organization, the leader started out in the Fire group. However, midway into the exercise I heard a lot of laughter. He was expelled from his group and assigned to the Earth group.

When I asked him what happened, he answered, "They started making their list and had gotten all the way to eleven reasons why they were the most awesome element, and I said, 'You guys are not following instructions. She said five to seven reasons—not eleven.' To which the group replied in unison, 'You're an Earth! Go over there.'"

I also noted that the Earth group had carefully come up to me and asked for a list of all the positive characteristics of each element. They wanted to do it "right."

Well, as you can imagine, the groups became very creative with their answers. Fires shouted out, "We are hot. We are exciting. We make things happen. We refine things. We illuminate the truth. In fact, we *are* the truth."

Waters replied, "We are the most awesome element because we get along with everyone. We can change things from solid to liquid or back again. We help things grow, and nothing could live without us."

Winds' reasons were as follows: "Wind is the most awesome element because we keep things moving. We are the first ones to bring you the scent of danger or the scent of spring. We are the only element that sees everything, and we are inspiring."

Earths said, "We are the most awesome element because without us none of you would have a place to stay. We can take little seeds and grow them into huge trees. Our work is mysterious and invisible and deep, and we are the only one of you that is solid ground."

At a seminar with leaders in Indianapolis, the creative Fire group elected a leader to demonstrate their superiority. He called one member from each of the other three elements and asked them to hold hands, which they did. Meanwhile, he stood in the center directing them. He then asked them to move slowly in a circle.

As they began to follow directions, he said, "This is it, folks. Every element in the world revolves around us." The group quickly disbanded and began throwing things at him as he made his way triumphantly back to the cheering Fires.

The Waters, not to be outdone, sent one of their representatives to speak. She smiled as she walked to the center of the room and invited the Fire representative to come up with her. Always eager to be the center of attention, the Fire obliged. As he drew near her, smiling at her recognition, she simply leaned over and picked up a pitcher of water and began to move toward him. He turned and made a hasty retreat to his corner. The entire room erupted in hoots and howls of laughter. She stood there smiling and said, "Who is the most awesome element? I think we have made our point."

The second part of the exercise is equally fun and revealing. I ask the elements to reveal what most bugs them about the opposite element, with Earths being the opposite of Winds, and Waters being the opposite of Fires. By now, people are usually warmed up and getting into it. I tell them to make the list of "bugnesses" personal.

In one group when the Earths rose to read what most bugged

them about the Winds, they said, "What bugs us the most about you Winds is that you are so flighty. You are always changing your mind. You can't sit still for a moment. You hardly ever complete what you started, and you are sometimes just plain silly."

The Winds replied, "You Earths are sticks-in-the-mud. You always have to have paperwork and documentation before you move—if you ever move on anything. You can't take a joke. And how shall we say this? What is that process when you keep drilling a hole in the ground? Oh, yes, we think the word is *boring!*"

Then the Waters addressed the Fires: "You Fires are so combustible. You think everything has to be done right now, and you don't listen to others. You always have to be the center of attention and think your way is the only way. You look at everything and everyone as fuel, and don't seem to care that sometimes you burn people in the process."

At that particular juncture I leaned forward and asked the Fire group: "How do you feel about what the Waters just said to you?"

As one, they smiled and gave each other high fives and said, "And their problem with that was what?"

Then the Fires got to address the Waters: "You folks are wishy-washy. You never take a direct path to anything. You avoid confrontation like the plague. You are always thinking of other people's feelings—so much so that no work can get done. You never take a stand, and you evaporate the minute things get hot."

People were laughing and yet a little uncomfortable at the truths that had been revealed. One man pleaded quietly (from the Water group, in fact), "I think we all need a group hug right now."

However, the healing was about to begin. I said, "Now, let's take each element that you just dissed, and write down five to seven things you admire and appreciate, even need, them for."

The groups set to work. The Fires finished quickly, as did two other groups, but the Waters kept writing and writing and writing. When I pointed out to them with some amusement that they had no trouble writing down the good qualities of others, they said, "Hey, this is who we are. We always see the good in others." And they kept writing.

Basically the Fires appreciated the Waters for being so thoughtful and reflective, and for coming in and cleaning up the messes they sometimes left behind in their zeal. The Waters appreciated the Fires for being so bold, exciting, and dynamic—and for being willing to confront others when necessary without fear.

The Winds appreciated the Earths for being so solid, grounded, and steady, as well as for giving them a place to play. The Earths appreciated the Winds for being exciting, for keeping things interesting, and for sharing their new ideas with them.

At the end of the exercise, everyone feels great. "Now, the final task," I say, "is that you are assigned to change the world. You have three minutes to assemble your team."

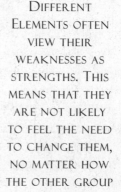

People move quickly, trying to determine which elements they need in order to be successful. Invariably I will find a group of two or three Fires standing in their same corner. I'll ask, "Couldn't you find anybody else to join your team?" And they will look at me with all seriousness and say, "We *are* the team!"

DIFFERENT ELEMENTS OFTEN VIEW THEIR WEAKNESSES AS STRENGTHS. THIS MEANS THAT THEY ARE NOT LIKELY TO FEEL THE NEED TO CHANGE THEM, NO MATTER HOW THE OTHER GROUP VIEWS THEM.

Whenever the opposing element gives the sometimes substantial litany of what it perceives to be huge failings, the elements being addressed invariably smile and nod and sometimes even thump their chests and shout, "Yes!" or "All right!"

Invariably they see these "failings" as what absolutely makes them powerful. In other words, they view their weaknesses as strengths. This means that they are not likely to feel the need to change them, no matter how the other group views them. The implication of this tendency is seen every day as conflicts arise over differences in style, with each party digging in to deliver more of the same rather than explore new ways of relating.

Getting Astounding Results

I then instructed each elemental grouping: "Please finish this sentence: If you really want to see awesome performance and astounding results from me, give me these four things . . ."

Following are their replies:

- The Winds asked for empowerment, support, trust, and freedom.

- The Earths asked for resources, commitment, balance, clear priorities, and trust.

- The Waters asked for freedom, guidance, expectations, opportunity, and patience.

- The Fires asked for freedom to act and control, acknowledgment, independence, challenges, and time.

I turned to the other elements and asked, "What do you think would happen if you gave them these things?"

What amazed me was that *every element* said, "They would be dangerous! We can't give them what they're asking for! It would throw us out of balance." Yet when I reminded them that the end result, as promised from each element, was awesome performance and astounding results, the elements began to think a little bit differently.

If you are a team leader and you give your Fires more control, they may astound you with amazing results. If you give the Waters more guidance, they promise to astound you with amazing results. If you give the Winds more freedom, they promise to bring you awesome performance. And if you give the Earths more resources and commitment, they will give you astounding results.

WHEN WORKING WITH EARTHS

Here is a summary of things to keep in mind when you work with the elements on your team.

- Give them time to do their work.

- Leave them alone to do their work.

- Give them lots of documentation and factual support.

- Allow them to create and/or provide them with design, structure, and order.

- Do probe carefully for hidden anger or resentment spots.

- Do include them in any major or long-term project.

Team them with Waters for growth, Winds for new ideas, and Fires for forward motion.

WHEN WORKING WITH WATERS

- Remember that relationships and the feelings of others are their core values.

- Allow them time for reflection and "detoxification."

- Allow them to find their own way to get there, once you've set the general guidelines for tasks.

- Listen to their subtle voices and suggestions.

- Do encourage them, see them, and treat them as vital team leaders (remember that nothing grows without them).

Team them with Fires for passion, Earths for long-range implementation, and Winds for diffusion and helping ideas get a jump start.

When Working with Winds

- Keep them stimulated.
- Don't box them in with single projects, rules, procedures, or details.
- Give them motion and flexibility.
- Listen to their new ideas, no matter how crazy they seem.
- They are the messenger element and can see the whole picture like no other element can.

Team them with Fires for exciting messaging, Waters for public relations, and Earths for follow-through.

When Working with Fires

- Give them authority as soon as possible.
- Challenge them with big, "impossible" tasks.
- Praise them constantly.
- Remind them of their need for the other Elements.
- Remember their highest need is achievement.

Team them with Earths for results, Winds for movement, and Waters for balance.

Following are some additional examples of how the different elements view one another.

"You Fires Never Admit You're Wrong"

In a team meeting of eleven strategic thinkers, the elements were asked what bugged them most about their opposite element and given fifteen minutes to vent. The opposite element of Fire is Water, and after the Fires unloaded on the Waters, the Waters' initial response was, "We don't want to say anything against the Fires because it might hurt their feelings."

When I as the facilitator pressed them to vent anyway, one of the quiet ones leaped to his feet and said, "I could be afraid because my boss here is a Fire. But if we can't be honest in this session, it is not going to do any of us any good." He took a deep breath and then plunged in: "You Fires take off in a direction and say, 'We are going to take this field!' You don't listen to any differing opinions or other ideas. You just charge on. Then, you end up in the middle of the field, realizing that you shouldn't be there, and proceed to yell at anyone who wasn't fully committed to the charge. 'Why aren't you out here with us?' you yell, even though you are starting to realize you shouldn't be there yourselves. And never, ever, ever do you admit you were wrong to go there in the first place!" With that said, he stood there trembling.

I asked the Fires how they felt about what he said, and their response was, "So?" Laughter broke out in the room, yet everyone there could feel the truth in what had been expressed.

The next exercise required the elements to express three things that they appreciated about their opposites.

This same Water stood up with tears in his eyes and said, "My mother was dying of liver cancer, and you Fires told me to go tend to her and you would cover for me. And when I was feeling so much pressure about everything, you comforted me and told me I would make it through. You got me through the night." He stopped talking and began to sob.

Every strength has a corresponding weakness, and this exercise demonstrated both the strength and weakness of Fire.

A Conflict-Resolution Tip

When there is conflict in a situation, a diagnostic tool I've come up with is this: Look for CAT1 and CAT2.

The *C* in CAT1 stands for *communication*. Assuming there is goodwill between the parties in dispute, nine out of ten times the problem is a communication breakdown. Instructions were not clear perhaps, or objectives were prioritized differently. Tardiness could occur because a phone call or memo was not received, for example, rather than an outright attempt to be rude. Always look first to see if and where communication broke down.

A stands for *alignment*. Are the parties involved *really* in alignment around the goals and objectives, or is there mouth "yes" and actions "no" behavior going on? If there is no alignment, the sooner *C* (communication) takes place around it, the better.

Note: Watch Earths and Waters particularly on this one, and don't assume just because they are there that they are behind you. In their tendencies to avoid confrontation they may not reveal their true feelings. Waters and Earths are prone to passive-aggressive behavior; they might say yes while their actions are ultimately going to say no.

The *T* in CAT1 stands for *trust*. What is the level of trust between the parties? When and where and if it is low, all manner of disputes, disruptions, and disease will occur. Trust is the invisible entity that can hold a team together against incredible odds. When it is lacking, however, any obstacle will be enough to alter or halt the journey.

CAT1: Diagnosis
Communication
Alignment
Trust

The solution in conflict is to look for CAT2.

In this case, the *C* stands for *change*. What needs to change here?

The *A* stands for *action*. What new actions will take place?

And the *T* in CAT2 stands for *time*. When exactly will the next action take place?

CAT2: Solution
Change
Action
Time

TEAM DYNAMICS

One CEO that I worked with is a Water, yet her schedule is that of an Earth. "Sylvia" is booked from meeting to meeting nonstop, and she is constantly being called upon to submit documentation and reports. She confessed to me that she was at the point where she didn't want to show up for work anymore, yet didn't know who to tell.

I took the profile of her and her assistant, Karen, who happens to be an Earth. We had a long dialogue about the need for this Water CEO to have more time for reflection and interaction with people. The assistant and I sat down and literally went through Sylvia's upcoming calendar for the next year, giving her one free/processing day between every day of meetings. Once Karen understood that Sylvia would function better with a looser schedule, the assistant used her Earth boundary-making skills to help Sylvia start to say no to multiple, draining requests on her time. Whereas before Karen was programming Sylvia according to her values and need for structure, she now became the guardian of this Water CEO's free time and need for reflection.

This organization was on the verge of losing a key leader due to a schedule and a pace that were not in line with her elementary nature. Imagine what the cost would have been had she just slowly faded away.

Following are tips to help you, as a team leader, better understand the needs and values of your team's elements.

If You Are a Team Leader of Water

Remember that these individuals generally:

- are motivated toward stability and compassion

- are oriented toward people and relationships

- prefer predictability; take action slowly and enjoy being team players; seek agreement, consensus, and balance

- tend to provide encouragement and support to others; defer to authority; rely on more traditional methods and techniques

- are capable of great adaptability, loyalty, and self-sacrifice; have excellent listening skills

- are seen by others as loyal, cooperative, patient, steady, and calm

- make decisions based on the general good after seeking all viewpoints and encouraging cooperation

If You Are a Team Leader of Water/Earth

Remember that these individuals generally:

- are motivated toward safety and harmony

- are oriented toward people and task completion

- prefer to move at a steady pace, engaging in activities that are predictable and procedural; work in a team atmosphere; see practical closure to tasks

- tend to be cautionary, compliant, respectful of authority, patient, indecisive, self-disciplined, and self-protective

- are capable of bringing order out of chaos; provide wise and conscientious counsel; absorb the stress of others; make careful preparation for any engagement

- are seen by others as supportive, loyal, stable, orderly, self-sacrificing, analytical, efficient, unemotional, patient, and good listeners
- make decisions based on the apparent well-being and safety for all

If You Are a Team Leader of Water/Wind

Remember that these individuals generally:

- are motivated toward optimism and energy
- are oriented toward people
- prefer moving reasonably quickly but setting their own pace; enjoy variety and sensory experiences, helping others; seek predictability and safety
- tend to ignore boundaries, express emotion, are open to new ideas, trust others, spread themselves too thin
- are capable of persuasiveness, idealistic trust, imaginative practicality, versatility, humor
- are seen by others as loyal, supportive, exciting, spontaneous (but not impulsive), energetic, optimistic, disorganized, warm, friendly, encouraging
- make decisions based more on emotion than on logic

If You Are a Team Leader of Water/Fire

Remember that these individuals generally:

- are motivated toward goals and accomplishment
- are oriented toward people
- prefer stability and predictability; like to set their own pace; enjoy action more than talking; promote completion of tasks and team efforts
- tend to display occasional stubbornness and inflexibility

Following are some quick identifiers (as well as positive team traits) of different element combinations involving Water.

WATER DESCRIPTIVE ELEMENT COMBINATIONS

Water/Wind	Water/Fire	Water/Earth
steady support	cautious flexibility	calm consistency
harmonious negotiation	quiet energy	tolerant observation
supportive loyalty	clear communication	reflective conscientiousness
cooperative expression	benevolent ingenuity	tranquil evolution
compassionate acceptance	quiet intensity	irresistible logic
versatile motion	buoyant warmth	tranquil stability
supportive friendliness	rhythmic transformation	harmonious diplomacy
practical imagination	cleansing renewal	adaptable diversity

Wind

These individuals generally:

- are motivated toward visible impact and immediacy
- are oriented toward people
- prefer to move at a fast pace; enjoy using verbal skills to influence; often ignore boundaries or chains of hierarchy; seek variety; are conscious of status and popularity; prefer working with people and having fun
- tend to be persuasive, extroverted, spontaneous, energetic, idealistic, trusting, restless and easily bored, inspiring
- are capable of exaggeration, emotional appeal, impulsivity, skillful networking

- are seen by others as engaging, optimistic, enthusiastic, friendly, talkative, humorous, disorganized and haphazard, observant
- make decisions based more on emotion than on logic

Wind/Fire

These individuals generally:

- are motivated toward goals and results
- are oriented toward people
- prefer to move at a fast pace, interacting with many people (large groups) and motivating them to action with persuasion and conviction; prefer immediate action to strategic planning; enjoy dramatic, widespread change; seek control; enjoy surmounting obstacles and overcoming challenges; seek physical activity
- tend to be volatile and impatient with obstacles; are directive with others, emotional, more likely to initiate projects than to finish them
- are capable of skillful networking; directly confront problems; have sharp evaluation of results; use storytelling as a powerful motivator; tolerate high levels of stress
- are seen by others as passionate, friendly, gregarious, communicative, optimistic, visionary, competitive, pioneering, willing to take calculated risks
- make decisions based on the big picture and evaluation of results

Wind/Earth

These individuals generally:

- are motivated toward creativity and results
- are oriented toward people and acceptance
- prefer fast-paced activity laced with quiet periods; have a strong drive to reach goals by getting the job done right based on facts and data; seek intellectual stimulation
- tend to overcommit; appreciate but have difficulty establishing and maintaining order; seek recognition and acceptance; postpone work in favor of socializing; experience inner turmoil or conflicted drive; are respectful of authority
- are capable of holding self and others to high standards; absorb and remember facts, data, and odd bits of information; probe for the "what if" factor when included in general planning and decision making
- are seen by others as exciting, spontaneous, energetic, analytical, efficient, outspoken
- make decisions based more on emotion than on logic
- make decisions after considering the implication for change on others

Wind/Earths are unusual combinations since they are the matchup of opposing elements. Being torn between a desire for change and a desire for stability, they will often pair up with complementary elements and take lesser leadership roles.

Wind/Water

These individuals generally:

- are motivated toward immediate results
- are oriented toward people
- prefer to move quickly; solve personal and work-related problems in practical ways
- tend to be responsive to the needs of others; forgive easily and quickly; lose focus and have difficulty prioritizing
- are capable of open and sensitive communication; have great versatility in life and the workplace; are adaptable to change and support others through change; are capable of patiently talking through conflict
- are seen by others as friendly, extroverted, optimistic, funny, energetic, spontaneous, exciting, idealistic, trusting, encouraging, patient
- make decisions after considering the implication for change on others

Wind/Waters are relationship-oriented types. They do well whenever a relationship needs to be encouraged, created, nurtured, or moved along. Winds and Waters love movement. (Think ocean.) They are driven not by results but more by "beingness" and enjoyment.

One YMCA director we worked with hit his forehead and said, "Now that I know this, I never should have sent Elise and Mandy to the regional conference." When I asked him why, he said, "Because they are both Wind and Water. They came back after one week and told us what a great time they had, and were going on and on about all the people they met. When I asked them what the program was about, they couldn't even remember. When I asked them what the agenda was, one of them looked at the other and said, 'What agenda?' Next time I am going to send an Earth with them for sure!"

Following are some quick identifiers (as well as positive team traits) of different element combinations involving Wind.

WIND DESCRIPTIVE ELEMENT COMBINATIONS

Wind/Fire	Wind/Earth	Wind/Water
restless passion	optimistic logic	volatile passion
dynamic catalyst	expressive objectivity	mercurial excitement
persuasive intensity	spontaneous creativity	restless versatility
creative energy	positive realism	lighthearted diplomacy
lyrical outspokenness	swift resourcefulness	lavish imagination
influential gregariousness	enigmatic modesty	creative negotiation
		generous mediation
		ambitious innovation

Fire

These individuals generally:

- are motivated toward control and achievement
- are oriented toward tasks and activity
- prefer to have authority, control, and leadership; prefer to change the status quo, to take risks, to enjoy competition, and may enjoy conflict (because conflict is engagement)
- tend to seek fast-paced, creative, and action-oriented environments
- are capable of complex multitasking, tolerating high levels of stress, and usually of delegating tedious details to others

- are seen by others as bold, direct, confident, competitive, pioneering, assertive, frank
- make decisions based on desired results

Fire/Earth

These individuals generally:

- are motivated toward order and efficiency
- are oriented toward tasks and activity
- prefer strategic planning with a strong drive to reach goals by getting the job done right leading to precise, accurate, high-quality outcomes
- tend to take calculated risks, act quickly, enjoy competition and challenge
- are capable of great attention to detail but likely to delegate management of details to others; understand the uses of power and will use it strategically; are able to act quickly but may exercise more caution than Fires
- are seen by others as confident, direct, capable, bold, analytical, controlling, impatient, critical, stubborn, visionary, intense, competitive
- make decisions based on bottom-line results

Fire/Earths have a tendency to be self-driven workaholics. Think Sherman tanks. Once Fire/Earths have set their minds on a task, nothing will stop them from accomplishing it. Fire/Earths are almost self-sustaining in that they have the drive to achieve with the knowledge of how to implement long-range sustainable tactics. Because they are motivated almost totally by results, they can often run over people and harm relationships in the process.

They also are prone to low-level listening skills and sometimes foolhardy stubbornness.

I read an article about a man in Phoenix who has been fighting a city traffic ticket for seventeen years. The $25 ticket has cost him about $23,000 in legal fees and untold costs for the city as it responds to all of his court documents. When asked why he didn't just pay the fine, he replied, "It's the principle of the thing." Fire/Earths are driven by principle—sometimes to their own detriment.

Fire/Water

These individuals generally:

- are motivated toward steadiness and results
- are oriented toward people and tasks
- prefer to set their own pace and get jobs done by steady, persistent effort
- tend to lead more by example than direction; measure results in terms of team effort; value continued learning
- are capable of better than average communication skills including effective listening skills and diplomacy
- are seen by others as bold, direct, confident, pioneering, assertive
- make decisions based on results gained from cooperative effort

Fire/Waters are interesting combinations because they can have a tendency to put themselves out. In an immature state Fire/Waters can be silly and volatile, forget proper boundaries, and cause great destruction. (Note the term fire/water in itself is often related to alcohol.) Yet in a mature form Fire/Waters can be great and passionate reformers. They often feel passionately about causes that need reform, yet go about the reform in nonshowy or nonviolent ways.

Mother Teresa, the dedicated social worker in India, was able to gain worldwide attention for her work with the poor and dying, always while remaining ultimately gentle and humble in her methods. I believe that Mahatma Gandhi was a Fire/Water, mobilizing an entire culture to shake off years of imperialism, yet doing so with humble methods and words, and being willing to take, but not deliver, the blows.

Fire/Wind

These individuals generally:

- are motivated toward activity and goals
- are oriented toward the big picture
- prefer learning through experience and enjoy quick action and change
- tend to spontaneous and possibly emotional behaviors and responses; are better at starting projects than finishing them
- are capable of using humor and charm to temper direct, bottom-line communication in order to inspire or motivate others
- are seen by others as fun, productive, outgoing, assertive, optimistic, confident, bold
- make decisions based on the big picture

Fire/Winds are messengers and "movers and shakers." They are the ones who want change and want it now. They have to see things in motion in order to feel they are accomplishing something.

If nothing changes as a result of their work, they view themselves as failures and will move on to new territories where there are new fuel sources present. Fire/Winds are volatile, easily offended, like to spout off, and yet can also be utterly charming and civilized.

Fire/Winds are often politicians, public speakers, actors or actresses, and entertainers. They are often the centers of attention as well as the causes of crises. If you want to see Fire/Winds at their most calm, throw them into a crisis situation and watch them settle into an almost supernatural calm. (Just make sure they didn't cause the crisis in order to be able to respond to it.)

Following are some quick identifiers (as well as positive team traits) of different element combinations involving Fire.

FIRE DESCRIPTIVE ELEMENT COMBINATIONS

Fire/Wind	Fire/Water	Fire/Earth
brilliant energy	determined steadiness	confident proficiency
joyful spontaneity		focused diligence
playful sensuality	dynamic diplomacy	restless caution
cleansing strength	confident adaptability	intrepid realism
bold vision		forged purpose
simmering dynamism	enterprising achievement	visionary analysis
passionate idealism	persistent steadiness	focused objectivity
assertive cooperation	patient arbitration	intense conscientiousness
	assertive practicality	
	bold influence	

Earth

These individuals generally:

- are motivated toward order and stability

- are oriented toward tasks and results

- prefer order, structure, procedure, consistency, data and closure, solitude

- tend to gather information, then follow a plan slowly and methodically to complete tasks within specific time frames; establish and maintain a neat, well-organized environment; respect authority and consequences; demonstrate compliance with procedures and guidelines

- are capable of working independently; exercise great curiosity; create impeccable organizational systems; give equal consideration to minute details and to overall outcome
- are seen by others as dependable, predictable, stable, logical, realistic and practical, critical, conscientious, cautious, objective, disciplined
- make decisions based on objective analysis of facts or data

Earth / Water

These individuals generally:

- are motivated toward order and stability
- are oriented toward people
- prefer order, structure, efficiency, but this is tempered by a focus on helping, encouraging, and supporting others and achieving balance
- tend to pursue or specialize in branches of various occupations where they can enjoy the direct benefit to others of their efforts and where positive feedback and approval for their efforts are provided
- are capable of adapting to a wider variety of situations than Earths and process information slowly and thoroughly; work on one project at a time
- are seen by others as loyal, supportive, calm, organized, logical, analytical, predictable
- make decisions by responding to situations objectively while also considering the needs of others

Earth/Wind

These individuals generally:

- are motivated toward stability and achievement
- are oriented toward people and idealism
- prefer stability and order, structure, procedure, consistency and organization; may prefer to move quickly at times; are less patient with repetitive activity
- tend to move cautiously, but often struggle with a desire to act quickly, intuitively
- are capable of being open to new ideas; occasionally ignore boundaries; sometimes send mixed signals; can provide strong and inspirational leadership
- are seen by others as enthusiastic, persuasive, creative, and idealistic; able to be objective, analytical, factual
- make decisions from an emotional basis

Earth/Fire

These individuals generally:

- are motivated toward stability and achievement
- are oriented toward tasks and results
- prefer to create careful plans, follow validated procedures, systems, or processes
- tend to get things done relying on strategies and procedures that are proven, constant, basic
- are capable of seeing the big picture and are flexible when evaluation of results indicates a change might be in order; are able to confront problems directly; can go from slow to overdrive in an instant

- are seen by others as bold, confident, directing, competitive, humorous, charming, and controlling

- make decisions based on hard results

Following are some quick identifiers (as well as positive team traits) of different element combinations involving Earth.

EARTH DESCRIPTIVE ELEMENT COMBINATIONS

Earth/Wind	**Earth/Water**	**Earth/Fire**
organized dynamism	generous support	logical objectivity
observant optimism	fertile practicality	abundant energy
communal sociability	persistent loyalty	accurate focus
consistent trust	consistent calm	abundant confidence
confident idealism	predictable serenity	direct communication
balanced gregariousness	solid encouragement	reliable decisiveness
analytical creativity	calm dependability	diligent achievement
consistent achievement	objective pragmatism	

A SIMPLE WAY TO HANDLE ALL THE ELEMENTS

Conflict will arise in any noble endeavor—especially when you have been wise enough to build diverse elements on your team.

It is very challenging to understand the values and desires of elements other than ourselves. It takes hours of devoted observation and practice. Yet my friend Lee Ellis offered a simple solution for the elements to handle each of the others, whether in conflict, pacing, or divergent thinking. He sums it up in one word: humility.

To his great insight, I have added three other *H* words to create what we on our team call the 4H solution to conflict. The four *H*'s are honor, humility, humor, and high calling.

Honor

Honor the points of view of others. They have unique and valuable perspectives to offer the team, even if right now you cannot see them or do not agree with them. Treating others with respect even in conflict will help move the team forward more quickly once a resolution has been identified. In *Jesus, CEO* I tell the tale of the prophet Balaam, who decided that since work was slow, he would take a commission to curse a competitor's town.

When the donkey he was riding refused to move forward on the trail, Balaam proceeded to beat the donkey until he suddenly saw an angel standing on the path. The angel informed Balaam that he was sent to slay him for disobedience to his high calling, but the donkey saved him because he kept him from going forward on an ill-conceived mission. The balking donkey was a team member that actually saved Balaam's life. Even though Balaam was the one in charge, the donkey saw what he couldn't and saved his life. I have had no fewer than fifty people across the country write and tell me that story affected their perspective on their team members almost more than any other. We need to honor and respect the viewpoints of others, no matter how ridiculous they may seem in their protest.

Humility

Humble yourself. Admit to others, and especially yourself, that you do not have all the answers, and you are willing to *seek* the truth, not *be* the truth, with the rest of the team. I will never forget reviewing the mission statement of an officer at Annapolis, who wrote that his mission was simply to "surrender to wisdom." This officer happened to be the highest-ranking one on the team, yet he saw his task as being willing to surrender to wisdom.

My friend Jackie Brewton grew up in Georgia as one of nine

children in an African-American family. Her mother worked three jobs and never took welfare in raising her clan, even after her husband died. Jackie and her siblings learned early that there were to be no excuses for pride or for blaming others.

She said she remembers coming home from school one day, after being called a racial name, and running to her mother. Her mother, rather than excoriating the person uttering it, told Jackie to immediately get down on her knees and pray for that poor person's ignorance to be turned to light. Jackie laughed as she told the story and said, "We learned early on not to bring other people's shortcomings to Mama because it would be *our knees* that would pay!"

Humor

Humor is a great reducer of mountains. Look for what might be funny in the situation if viewed years down the road, and then decide to laugh about it now. I remember a story a friend told me. One of his young team members was furious about a deadline. Feeling that the work required was too much too soon, the team member walked into the supervisor's office and threw the report on the desk and then stormed out.

"What did you do?" I asked in shock. Knowing this supervisor to be a Wind/Fire, I fully expected her to say that the team member was "fired on the spot."

"Well, knowing my element, I took the weekend to cool down. I also realized that this young recruit was a Wind/Fire as well, so I could appreciate his tendency to lose control under pressure and try to place the blame somewhere else. I also knew this young individual has the potential to someday run this company, so I did not want to make a hasty decision that could cost him his career. I then called him up and asked him to review what his needs were in the organization as he had an opportunity now to explore other options.

"When he came into my office the next Monday, deeply apologetic and trembling at what my response would be, I quietly took a piece of paper and began to show him how to construct a paper airplane, saying that next time he might want to add some aero-dynamics to the toss. When he saw that I was able to see some humor in the situation, he calmed down, and we had a great dis-cussion about how things worked in this particular team."

Who can forget President Ronald Reagan's great gift of humor to the nation that was in near panic over his assassination attempt? "Honey, I forgot to duck," he said to his wife, Nancy, when she was allowed to see him in the hospital. As the doctors nervously gath-ered to remove the bullet from his body, he looked up at them and said, "Please tell me you are all Republicans," before he went under the anesthesia. His ability to see humor in a life-or-death situation greatly reduced the anxiety of the team assembled to save his life.

High Calling

If we remember that all people have a high calling to fulfill, it becomes apparent that we are put here to lovingly help them find it. One might say that the true mark of a leader is inspiring and iden-tifying the high calling in others. Jesus demonstrated this when he called formerly flaky Simon "my rock" and encouraged people of humble background and means to be "the light of the world."

How to Enhance Your Value to Your Boss

As we discussed earlier, according to *Fast Company* magazine's Leadership Initiative Survey, one of the top three things that keeps CEOs up at night is "being aware of the latest news and trends." In fact, 97 percent of the CEOs surveyed ranked this as their number one "late night" concern.

So, if you are a Wind, you are naturally suited to scanning the environment and climate for changes. Send your boss clippings of articles or bits of information you gather from your mental or physical wanderings, and you will be perceived as a valuable mem-ber of the team.

To get financing for his voyage, for example, Christopher

Columbus harnessed his Windy desire for travel with Queen Isabella's Earth/Fire desire for Catholic converts. He promised to bring her new spices as well, adding sensual imagery to a woman hungry for more territory.

The number two concern of the CEOs in the survey was "getting the best prices on supplies."

Here is where the Earth in you can shine. Do field research and uncover new resources. Crunch the numbers and do an exhaustive comparison model, simplified, and you will be held in good stead.

If you are a Water, you can use your diplomacy and relationship skills to quietly integrate the merits of your boss's new policies, or help explain to others her idiosyncrasies. Become an expert on the needs and values of others, and present them to your boss in such a way that she sees the merit in meeting their needs as well as advancing her new agenda.

While living overseas, Wind/Water Benjamin Franklin used humor, charm, laughter, and the love of wine to persuade the French to send aid to the struggling American armies. One could say he had them literally laughing all the way to *our* bank.

If you are a Fire, you can use your desire for reform to help point out areas that need improvement, and offer practical solutions that involve putting yourself in charge and thereby "taking the heat."

To summarize key understandings, consider the following:

For advancement . . .

- If your boss is an Earth, bring her documentation.
- If your boss is a Water, bring him new tools for relationships.
- If your boss is a Wind, bring him adventure and excitement.
- If your boss is a Fire, bring her obedience and more fuel.

In order to serve your boss better . . .

- If your boss is an Earth, help her free up more time for analysis.
- If your boss is a Water, help him make decisions quickly.
- If your boss is a Wind, handle the details.
- If your boss is a Fire, give him praise, attention, and loyalty, and you will shine.

4

How to Grow (and Retain) Your Team

"No part of the productive resources of industry operates at a lower efficiency than human resources . . . The management of people should be the first and foremost concern of operating managements, rather than the management of things and techniques, on which so much attention has been focused."

—Peter F. Drucker[1]

A wise leader will use the elements to help grow and retain his or her team. Mastering the understanding of each element's values, needs, and desires will allow you to place them in situations where they can thrive and serve the largest good.

Wind Team Members

Generally speaking, your Wind team members will want new and exciting assignments with lots of freedom. Build in field trips whenever and wherever possible. Let them run errands to get out of the building, or put them in charge of relationships that require high engagement and lots of travel.

Key phrases that describe Winds might be: "Been there, done

that" or "Gotta run." Additional phrases might be: "What's new?" What's next?" and "I feel a little boredom coming on."

Water Team Members

Your Water team members will need lots of time for reflection and a conflict-free environment. They will want assignments that involve building deep and satisfying relationships over time, and they will want to be able to see the fruit of their efforts blossom and grow. Waters also will find their own way to accomplish tasks, often in faster and easier ways than you might have planned for or anticipated. If bottled up with no freedom of expression or time to reflect, they can become stagnant and even toxic.

Key phrases that describe Waters might be: "Can't we all just get along?" or "Whatever."

Earth Team Members

Your Earth team members will do well with high structure and order. Documentation is food for them. Tasks that are written out and can be accomplished in an orderly, timely, and fairly predictable fashion are high food. Earths may work slowly and may not show visible signs of excitement, yet they may be spinning one thousand miles per hour. Remember, the center of an Earth is always fire, so while the passion may not show, it does probably glow if the Earths stick with you on the team.

Key phrases that might come from Earths are: "You're late" or "I can't work in all this chaos." Additional phrases might be: "I need more research on this," or "Let's appoint a committee to study this more deeply."

Fire Team Members

Your Fire team members will want autonomy, authority, and control. They also have higher than average needs for recognition and constant praise or "tending to." Fires have a high need to be or feel that they are in charge. They do best when they have specific territories of control and when they are not left to themselves too long. Fires are the least likely element to have self-control, and they are prone to burnout, depression, and despair unless tempered by the other elements. Fires thrive in crisis, yet beware that they do not become the heroes of their self-created disasters. (A card I once bought for my redheaded niece read: "I can stay calm in a crisis because usually I am the cause of it.")

Fires need something they can improve, refine, reform, or change.

Fires abhor the status quo, and they are always looking for ways to make things better, newer, more current, shinier, or whatever state might make it evident that they have been on the scene.

In well-modulated settings Fires can bring tremendous comfort and illumination to others on the team. Fires are also capable of great warmth and sunshine.

Here are key phrases that might come from Fires: "Don't worry; I'm in charge here," or "Those rules apply to other people." Additional phrases might be: "My way or the highway," or "You're either with me or against me."

I was working with a start-up company that had only four employees. The CEO was a Fire/Earth with a very high drive to launch a new product and service into the community.

Surrounding him were two Waters and another associate who was also a Fire/Earth. One would have expected that the two Fire/Earths would have

> FIRES ABHOR THE STATUS QUO, AND THEY ARE ALWAYS LOOKING FOR WAYS TO MAKE THINGS BETTER, NEWER, MORE CURRENT, SHINIER, OR WHATEVER STATE MIGHT MAKE IT EVIDENT THAT THEY HAVE BEEN ON THE SCENE.

had a great rapport. However, the younger associate began not to thrive in the constant turmoil and uncertainty of the start-up atmosphere. He was always asking for more control over aspects of the program that he really liked. Unfortunately his Fire leadership potential did not have an Earth bridge to it; he continuously failed to return phone calls to the boss in a timely manner or show up for work on time. Finally the CEO had to let him seek employment elsewhere because of the young man's failure and inability to adapt to the flexibility and service attitude required in the organization at that phase.

Both Water associates flourished, however, easily adapting themselves to the needs and urgencies of the moment, thriving in their constantly and persistently being needed as they all watched the young organization grow.

Once you and your team members understand your own elements, the fun and value really begin to take place.

A CREATIVE SOLUTION

Three college professors used a creative, elemental approach to solve a common workplace issue. Their work is detailed in the *MIT Sloan Business Review* article "Unexpected Connections: Considering Employees' Personal Lives Can Revitalize Your Business."[2] A multiyear action grant from the Ford Foundation supported their work.

While they were probably unaware of it, I immediately recognized that their successful techniques represented an elemental approach to a management challenge.

A group of engineers, both men and women, was challenged to produce a new product on an extremely tight timetable, using technology that was unfamiliar to them and receiving no additional resources. Long hours after regular workdays and weekend work after that began to cause mounting stress. Members of the team found "they were working in a continual crisis mode."

The authors stepped back to look at the work patterns in general and study the underlying norms and processes that were occurring. They discovered that the workday was filled with many unnecessary and unproductive interruptions. They also began to understand why the unit worked that way even though it was generally understood to be inefficient: "For example, people noted that the norm was to reward individual heroics; someone would get kudos for solving a visible problem even if that person had caused it in the first place!"

The authors challenged the team to experiment with a new design. They divided the day to allow for "quiet times" and "interactive times." The result? This team achieved an on-time product launch *and* received several awards for quality! "They also reported feeling more in control of their own time, less stressed, and less likely to take work and worries home with them at night."

The new structure caused them to think twice before interrupting others: "Managers, trying to respect quiet time, reduced the number of status reports they requested, and found that this made the engineers more, not less, productive."

Analysis

From my perspective, researchers Bailyn, Fletcher, and Kolb used an Earth approach (studying the underlying processes) and discovered that the crisis mode of Wind and Fire was wearing everyone down. Constant interruption and distraction were commonplace. (Note that the Winds and Fires were being rewarded for solving crises they helped create.)

The authors reworked the structure (Earth) to allow for "quiet times" (Water) and "interactive times" (Wind). The result was better than anyone had expected, with the Fires on the team still being allowed to meet their deadlines and win awards.

The authors also challenged several long-held myths in business:

- More time invested in a project automatically leads to greater productivity.

- Time is an unlimited resource.

- The most committed workers are those who work the longest hours.
- Individual competition and heroics are the best ways to get the most out of people.

They stated, "When work is performed in an atmosphere of continual crisis or when the response to problems is to do the same thing, only harder, there are clear opportunities for innovation and change."

Use the Elements
to Cut Meeting Time in Half

In another case closer to home, I worked with the staff of a multi-million-dollar nonprofit agency. After doing their PEP assessments, the CEO and his vice president realized that they were Fires. "First we shook our heads," said the CEO, "and then we laughed. Our poor staffers! What have they had to endure all this time?"

I spent two hours going over each person's PEP report among the entire team. Two months later the CEO reported back to me: "Meetings that used to take us an hour now take fifteen minutes. The team knows what I need and am looking for, and I know they know how to get it." The CEO's secretary later took me aside and said, "I used to get so upset with him. Now I don't take things personally anymore. I just use my Water to calm him down and keep on rolling."

Use the Elements to Improve Productivity

A construction company in the West came to me with some team dynamic challenges. The employees worked in pairs. It seemed that some pairs were more productive than others, but the CEO couldn't figure out why. After a half day of training and having each team member take the PEP, the CEO learned that the less productive pairs contained only Waters, while the more productive pairs had a Wind or a Fire between them. The CEO shifted the two Waters so that each had a Wind or a Fire with him, and productivity went up.

USE THE ELEMENTS TO SETTLE CONFLICTS

A husband-and-wife team decided to open a greenhouse together. It was fun to watch their budding excitement as the opening drew near. "Susan," it seems, assumed that her husband, "Rob," would be there to help her from the time the shop opened until it closed. Six weeks into the opening, however, the two were at each other's throats. I offered to help them discover their elements, and the PEP assessment revealed that Susan was an Earth, while Rob was a Wind. He was understandably chafing at having to stay in one spot for twelve hours a day, while she was totally in her Earth element, a greenhouse. They devised a plan to allow Rob to run the errands, pick up the supplies, and do marketing in the surrounding area during the day, while she handled the in-house details of running the business. Once the changes were made, customers walked into a much more serene atmosphere.

In another true-to-life story, a friend had a party in her new home. It seems she had neglected to obtain a parking permit for each guest, and when a neighbor called the police to report all of the illegally parked cars, Elena went livid. Being a Fire, she decided to immediately confront the complaining neighbor. "This is ridiculous!" she fumed, irate that a neighbor should be so unreasonable. However, she wisely commandeered one of her gentler guests, Jasmine, to go along with her.

Jasmine, a Water, later related to me: "I was sweating so badly I could even feel it in my palms. I hate conflict! As Elena rang the doorbell, I looked around at his driveway before the neighbor opened the door and noticed that he had a Dallas Cowboys bumper sticker on his car. As soon as the door opened, I smiled at him and said, 'How about those Cowboys?' He suddenly launched into an exposition of why he loved the Cowboys so much, even though they never should have traded so-and-so. By the time we got around to the issue of the parking complaint, he said, 'Aw, that was nothing. I just didn't know what was going on.'"

Elena never had to say a word, which is a good thing, because according to her, she wanted to rip his head off. Knowing herself to be a Fire, she deliberately took along Jasmine, a Water, to help diffuse the situation and soothe the way.

Case Study: Which Elements Have the Following Work Styles?

A memo comes down from the head office, stating that Project Y has to be turned around quickly.

James says, "Okay, gang, let's get on this now. I propose we work through the weekend and do whatever it takes to make this thing happen. Let's meet at my house and start Friday night, work through Saturday, and try to finish this on Sunday. Maybe we can pull an all-nighter if we have to." Joan says, "Okay, whatever—I'll be there." Susan says, "I can't make the entire meeting, but I can drop off some information that I think you'll find really valuable. I can maybe pop in on Saturday for a few hours as well." Derek says, "There is really no reason why this project can't be delivered on time with us working on it during our regular working hours. Besides, we haven't even completed Project B yet."

- James is probably a _____ because . . .
- Joan is probably a _____ because . . .
- Susan is probably a _____ because . . .
- Derek is probably a _____ because . . .

Food for Thought
- Does this scenario sound familiar? Which members of your team remind you of James, Joan, Susan, or Derek; and why?
- Which Element can contribute most to this meeting?

Case Study: "So That's Why She Won't Take a Stand"

Two top executives of a very large company were interested in some of my programs. I met with them and began to explain the four elements PEP concept. They listened with growing interest as I gave example after example of people whose paradigms of understanding shifted once they "got it."

After I had gone through the characteristics of each element and how we all are different in that regard, one of the executives, Sheri, sat up straighter and said, "Wow! You just solved a major problem in my mind regarding Leila. I have a coworker who drives me crazy because I can never get her to take a stand. Now I know why she can't. She's Water!"

At that point we burst out laughing at the visual "truth" of what she described. Sheri continued with a raised eyebrow: "So, in order to utilize her greatest strengths, I should provide more direction and boundaries for her."

Two weeks later I got a report. Leila was thriving with Sheri's new leadership style: "I'm a confronter, and she's the diplomat. I can see now how we can make a great team. I used to just want to fire her, but now I harness her strengths to move my initiatives throughout the organization."

Then we laughed again at the metaphor because, as you probably guessed, Sheri is a Fire.

Food for Thought

- Why won't Water take a stand?

- If it were to "take a stand," what condition would it be in?

- Why might Leila be thriving and becoming more productive with Sheri's new leadership style?

Just for Fun

Which elements are most likely to be perceived as leaders and heroes?

Which two elements probably do most of the work?

Which elements are most naturally designed for transformation and change?

Hints and Helps

Earth can sometimes be hindered by its own overwhelming sense of responsibility to others.

Water can sometimes be hindered by its tendency to take the path of least resistance.

Wind can sometimes be hindered by its tendency to lose momentum and focus.

Fire can sometimes be hindered by its own brilliance.

Tips on the Elements

Earth identifies itself by what it supports.

Water identifies itself by what it grows.

Wind identifies itself by what it moves.

Fire identifies itself by the flame of its own passion.

OBSERVATIONS ON THE ELEMENTS

Earth

Earth seems to be moving slowly or not at all. Yet it is spinning at one thousand miles per hour.

Earth always seems to be calm and dispassionate on the outside. Yet the core of earth is fire.

Never attempt to build anything lasting or solid without an Earth on the team.

Water

Water is the most flexible of the elements—capable of changing into steam, rain, mist, ice, hail, or even delicate snowflakes.

Water is the second most abundant element on the planet.

Water can support multiple forms of life naturally and easily. (Think ocean.)

Water may seem to be the element least likely to get angry, but the world was destroyed once by a flood.

Wind

Wind is the only element that circles the globe and thus sees the biggest picture of all.

Wind is the only element that does not know it exists unless it sees the other elements responding to it.

Wind never looks back, so it is least likely to hold a grudge or assemble the family archives.

Every day is new to the Wind.

Whenever a Wind says something, listen but filter, giving the ideas a few days to settle before you act on them unless there is a warning of danger.

Fire

Fire cannot help being the center of attention. It just usually is.

Fire knows (but doesn't want you to know) that it is the most dependent of all the elements.

It cannot exist without the dual fuel of earth and wind.

Fire is considered the most civilizing of the elements—allowing us to protect ourselves, and heat and cook foods, thus ensuring survival.

Fire is the element most oriented to the present moment, thus causing it to be demanding of action—now.

POP QUIZ

1. Which two elements are most likely to want to be seen as the heroes?

    a. Earth   c. Wind
    b. Water   d. Fire

2. Which two elements are least likely to have work that "shows"?

    a. Earth   c. Wind
    b. Water   d. Fire

3. Which two elements are most likely to get their work done in a hurry?

    a. Earth   c. Wind
    b. Water   d. Fire

4. Which element looks the slowest but is actually overall moving the fastest?

    a. Earth   c. Wind
    b. Water   d. Fire

5. Which element is at the center of earth?

    a. Water   c. Fire
    b. Wind

6. Which element is the only one that covers the entire globe?

    a. Earth   c. Wind
    b. Water   d. Fire

7. Which element is the first one to sense danger and opportunity?

    a. Earth   c. Wind
    b. Water   d. Fire

8. Which element is the *most* flexible?

    a. Earth   c. Wind
    b. Water   d. Fire

9. Which element is the *least* flexible?

    a. Earth   c. Wind

    b. Water d. Fire

10. Which two elements are most likely to honor rules and procedures?

    a. Earth   c. Wind

    b. Water d. Fire

11. Which two elements are least likely to want to follow rules and procedures?

    a. Earth   c. Wind

    b. Water d. Fire

12. If you were forming a team that needed to move quickly, which elements would you select?

    a. Earth   c. Wind

    b. Water d. Fire

13. If you wanted a group that would be sure to get things done in an orderly and timely manner, which elements would you select?

    a. Earth   c. Wind

    b. Water d. Fire

14. You need to send someone out to "get a feeling" for an area. Which element(s) would you send? Justify your answer.

    a. Earth because . . .   c. Wind because . . .

    b. Water because . . .   d. Fire because . . .

15. Which two elements are the most naturally suited to long-term diplomacy?

    a. Earth   c. Wind
    b. Water   d. Fire

16. You need to get a message to a large number of people in difficult circumstances. You choose the following two elements:

    a. Earth because . . .   c. Wind because . . .
    b. Water because . . .   d. Fire because . . .

17. You come home and find that your Windy spouse is cranky. To help ease the situation, you:

    a. pull up a chair, sit down, and begin to analyze him/her
    b. come up with your own list of reasons to be cranky
    c. ignore him/her
    d. suggest that both of you go for a drive and talk

18. You come into work and your Fiery boss is in a fury. You handle the situation by:

    a. backing away and giving him/her time to cool off
    b. siding with him/her in the argument
    c. suggesting that the two of you go for a drive
    d. pulling up a chair, sitting down, and making a list

19. Your coworker is driving you crazy. You arrive consistently on time, but he drops in at ten and works till seven, comes in at noon and works till eight, or calls and says he is working at home that day. This behavior really upsets you. You feel he is irresponsible. Yet somehow this person manages to get the work done. You address the situation by:

a. recognizing that you are probably a _____ and that he is probably a _____.

b. complaining to your boss.

c. staying grumpy and burying your resentment.

20. You are planning an impromptu party. Match the best elements to the following tasks:

1. Earth
2. Water
3. Wind
4. Fire

a. Send the invitations.

b. Plan for the food.

c. Make sure people are seated next to the ones they'll most likely get along with.

d. Provide the entertainment.

Answers: 1. c, d;   2. a, b;   3. c, d;   4. a;   5. c;   6. c;   7. c;   8. b;   9. a;   10. a, b;   11. c, d;   12. c, d;   13. a, b;   14. b, c;   15. a, b;   16. c, d;   17. d;   18. a;   19. a (Earth, Wind);   20. 1) b; 2) c; 3) a; 4) d.

16–20 correct—You're great at this.

11–15 correct—You're catching on fast.

6–10 correct—Are you going with your gut?

1–5 correct—Are you really trying?

Having a basic understanding of what each Element needs and values can elevate conflict from an attack on personalities to a viewpoint of respecting and valuing core differences between people.

Ignoring or devaluing one Element at the cost of the others only and always leads to imbalance, and hence a lessening of overall productivity. You will be amazed at how this elemental understanding is going to shift how you view—and handle—conflict.

5

An Elemental Look
at Understanding
Your Customer

In his seminal book *Crossing the Chasm,* author Geoffrey Moore makes the point that high-tech companies falter(ed) by assuming that all customers were and are the same. He divides high-tech customers into four basic categories, which are "early adapters," "middle adapters," "later adapters," and "laggards."

The early adapters buy into innovative services or products simply because they are new. Functionality is not as important as being on the cutting edge and being seen as being on the cutting edge. Early adapters eagerly embrace whatever is new, hip, and different. Their enthusiasm leads the business owners into thinking that the entire world will be welcoming to the new product and service.

This belief is somewhat enforced by the phase-two customers, the middle adapters, who follow along the heels of the early adapters and buy according to the trends, quickly picking up and promoting the new product or service.

With two waves of eager customers under their belts, the new companies ramp up production, hire scads of marketing gurus, launch big advertising campaigns, and purchase expensive houses in the California hills. Alas, they soon discover that unless they did their homework on the third customer base, the "later adapters." they will not cross the chasm, but tumble into it, along with all their sweet dreams of success.

The significant and vital third wave of customers—the masses, if you will—does not have the same buying triggers as the early adapters. In fact, Moore states that they do not even value the references, referrals, or opinions of the first two groups, but view them as "somewhat dangerous."

MOST SALES AND MARKETING PEOPLE ARE WINDS AND FIRES, WHILE MOST PURCHASING GROUPS ARE EARTHS AND WATERS. UNDERSTANDING THE DIFFERENT VALUES OF EACH ELEMENT, AND COMMUNICATING THAT UNDERSTANDING IS VITAL TO ANY LONG-RANGE SALES EFFORT.

Relating this group of customers to the elements, I would say that the early adapters are the Winds, the second group is the Fires, the third group is the Earths, and the fourth and final group is the Waters. Let me expound on this a bit.

Winds are usually the first to scent and pick up a new trend or fashion. Most Winds that I know never met an idea they didn't like. One can observe the wind paying just as much attention to a tiny scrap of paper as it might to an elaborate hand-painted silken scarf.

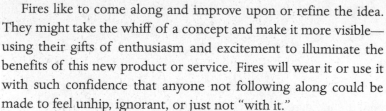

Fires like to come along and improve upon or refine the idea. They might take the whiff of a concept and make it more visible— using their gifts of enthusiasm and excitement to illuminate the benefits of this new product or service. Fires will wear it or use it with such confidence that anyone not following along could be made to feel unhip, ignorant, or just not "with it."

However, the third group, the Earths, do not care about trends or fashions. In fact, the newer or trendier something is, the less likely they are to adapt it. The buzz words that sound like honey to the Winds and Fires sound like alarm bells to the Earths and Waters, the "laggards." It is the gap between these two groups that Moore calls the chasm.

Unless strategists realize that there is a huge and significant difference in thinking between the early adapters (Wind/Fires) and the later users (Earth/Waters), millions of dollars' worth of time and momentum can be lost.

My observation is that most sales and marketing people are Winds and Fires, while most purchasing groups are Earths and Waters.

Understanding the different values of each element, and communicating that understanding, is vital to any long-range sales effort.

While word-of-mouth and viral marketing (note the Wind words) are every executive's dream, the truth is that unless and until the product or service takes root and begins to blossom and grow in the minds of the customers, no long-lasting, sustainable profits are made.

CASE STUDY ON BUSINESS

On September 15, 2004, the headline on the front page of the *Arizona Republic* read, "Univ. of Phoenix Pushes Ahead." The subhead read, "Federal audit doesn't slow aggressive growth efforts." Reporter Dawn Gilbertson wrote, "The University of Phoenix disputes the government's portrait that it sells education with the zeal of a hard-charging telemarketer, but recent memos to recruiters reveal tactics similar to those recently cited by federal regulators."

One of the e-mail memos the reporter had obtained read, "Get on the phones and be a part of this HUGE explosion of enrollments that will begin today and carry us through August!!!" (Which elements do you see in action here?)

The company, with student enrollments now topping two hundred thousand, had just settled a record $9.8 million fine with the U.S. Department of Education for its "corporate culture overly focused on boosting enrollment." (Which two elements are speaking here?)

Terri Bishop, senior vice president of public affairs, stated, "We don't apologize for being a sales organization at the University of Phoenix. We have always operated under the assumption that sales is part of what we do."

Another article by Judd Slivka on page two of that same newspaper, called "Reactions Differ Amid Large Student Body," detailed that some students had different opinions of the school. One student said that he liked the University of Phoenix experience so much that upon completion of his bachelor's degree, he returned for his master's degree. However, another student complained that her enrollment adviser had not told her that the degree program she wanted would take five years rather than the two and a half that were represented to her. "There's a lot of things she didn't tell me," she went on to say. Another student in the article said, "From the standpoint of classes, it's been great. However, from customer service, it's been very bad."

According to the article, the University of Phoenix, which is owned and run by the Apollo Group, "has been one of the best performers on Wall Street in the decade, with an 11,000 percent gain. On the news of the fine the stock fell slightly, to close down less than one percent."

Questions

- Based on this story, which two elements seem to be the driving force behind the school?
- Name four clue words in the article that support your choice.
- When the senior vice president responded to accusations of being overly aggressive, which two elements were most evident in his response?
- Based on two of the students quoted in the second article, which elements might be less dominant in the university's delivery system? Why?
- Which elements might the unhappy students be? Why?
- Federal fines notwithstanding, the university is a darling of Wall Street. Why?

- The federal regulators were probably which elements? Why?
- How might the two parties (the University of Phoenix) and (the U.S. Department of Education) use this event to learn from each other?

Answers and Food for Thought

The headline writers gave us a clue about the elements involved. Which element wants to "push ahead"?

"The zeal of a hard-charging telemarketer" presents the elements of Wind and Fire (even including the medium of choice, which is voice or wind oriented).

In the e-mail memo—"Get on the phones and be a part of this HUGE explosion of enrollments that will begin today and carry us through August!!!"—note the following:

- Fire's commanding and excitement-oriented tone.
- The writer is urging the readers to use the phone. Which element is that?
- The writer asking for A "HUGE explosion." Which elements get excited by that?
- Note also the Wind words "carry us through August!!!" (I particularly got a kick out of the three exclamation points that followed. Only a Wind/Fire would use those. They even look like little flames.)

The VP of public affairs used phrases like "we don't apologize," which is a Fire trait, and "we have always operated" this way, which is an Earth trait of defending and validating the status quo based on past actions.

If indeed some advisers are a little short on the details, what elements might they be operating under?

Customer service would imply that applying a bit more Earth in the details and the humility of Water might ease some of the complaints. The fact that the first student who complained did not get the details accurately indicates that she might be a Wind, dealing with a Wind or Water adviser. The fact that the second student who complained said the classes were great but the customer service was bad indicates she might be a Water (seeing both sides of the issue) mixed with Fire (being willing to be interviewed and complain).

The university is a darling of Wall Street because of its results. Wall Street historically values profits and has not been particular about how a company gets there. One might say it is thus a combination of Fire/Earth.

The federal regulators are probably Earths. One clue is that people who work in government organizations usually value stability. They also might be a combination of Earth/Fire because they are oriented toward justice and doing things right.

The University of Phoenix has been able to rise so quickly in part because other, more Earth/Water academic settings move so slowly. Most schools and academic settings require people to adjust their schedules to the way things are done and have always been done, whether or not it is convenient.

Thus, the Earthlike U.S. Department of Education could take a lesson in how to excite people about enrolling in school as well as encouraging more creative class scheduling.

Meanwhile, the Fire/Wind university is paying for the Earth lesson of making sure that it accounts carefully for how it is using federal aid.

There was another article that detailed how federal aid is apportioned and why a fine was levied, but it was full of graphs, numbers, and fine print. Being a Wind, I didn't want to take the time to cut it out and interpret the details.

CAN RELIGIOUS DIFFERENCES BE "ELEMENTAL"?

The man behind the scenes worked fifteen years to help establish a prayer breakfast in Congress. Without fanfare or publicity he managed to befriend world leaders of every denomination and religious persuasion, and he is often called upon for prayer and counsel, providing there are no cameras or publicity attached. This person believed and believes that the best way to preach the gospel is to be a friend to others, no matter who they are or what their needs are. He calls himself simply "a follower of Jesus," and does not claim to represent any denomination.

I was present at a meeting in Washington, D.C., where a group of people stood up and berated this person for not having the name of Jesus in the official prayer breakfast documents. They said, within my hearing as well as everyone else's in the room, that unless he reinserted the name of Jesus in the program and began openly having altar calls for commitments to Christ at the end of each prayer breakfast, this group was going to withdraw its support. The man calmly looked at them and said, "Do whatever you feel you must do," and he refused to get into an argument with them.

Food for Thought

- Most likely, what element is this unnamed man? Why?
- Most likely, what element is the group demanding the insertion of the name of Jesus in the program? Why?
- In your opinion, which party is honoring Jesus more? Why or why not?
- Where else in today's religious environment do you see these kinds of confrontations taking place? With what results?

My prayer is that examples like those I've shared in this chapter will give you valuable tools for discerning the "truth" in various situations and help broaden your perspective on how you view—and treat—those different from yourself.

6

CAREER IMPLICATIONS

In a September 6, 2004, informal phone-in study conducted by the *Arizona Republic* newspaper,[1] 70 percent of the people surveyed said they would leave a good-paying job for a job or career that they really loved, even if it paid less. This finding confirms an April 1990 *Boardroom Report* showing that more than 70 percent of all white-collar workers are dissatisfied with their jobs. According to the same report, 40 percent of white-collar workers stated "they would be happier working someplace else." More than 50 percent had recently updated their resumes, and more than 33 percent of the eleven hundred middle managers surveyed had been in touch with a job search company in the past six months.[2]

Career dissatisfaction runs high in the sales industry as well. One survey of five hundred salespeople discovered that 33 percent were on the verge of quitting their jobs, and another 40 percent were only moderately happy with their positions.

Lawyers aren't too happy either. The American Bar Association found that 25 percent of the three thousand lawyers it surveyed planned to change jobs in the next two years.[3]

While the stated purpose of education is, among other things, to help people find good careers, something isn't working. (I saw a T-shirt the other day in a Santa Fe gift shop that read, "A career is a job that has gone on too long.")

We live in changing times, and a tool that can help people plan fulfilling careers is "visioning." Yet one of the most neglected components of career planning is visioning. All too often as we face the vast horizon of the future, we focus only on skill sets. "What are you really good at?" we ask. And we test, and then we point. For example, one man put together a radio when he was a child, was praised, and went on to become an electronics engineer. As it turned out, what he really wanted to be all along was a counselor. Career planning is often all too hazy a guess, based on skills, that can send people in the wrong direction.

One way to help position you or your team in career planning is a simple exercise I use with clients.

You May Have Already Won!

Imagine that it is ten years from now. You have won the lottery, so money is not a concern for you. You are working at something you dearly love, and you are giving back to the community. Describe your ideal life in detail and in the present tense.

If you've never done that exercise, I suggest you do it right now. It can save you many wrong turns and detours as you use your imagination to create a compelling vision for yourself. We do this exercise, with amazing results, in our work with students and at-risk youth. (Log on to www.lauriebethjones.com for more information.)

Recently I was leading a Path4Teens program in the juvenile justice facility in my hometown. Seventeen first offenders, fifteen to seventeen years old, were gathered in the training room. I learned later that their offenses ranged from shoplifting to drug possession.

Needless to say, the teens were not a willing or an enthusiastic audience. There was almost no eye contact, most of them were slumped in their chairs, and two of them were actually asleep with their heads on the desks. I introduced myself and my assistants, and I kept praying, *Dear Lord, please just let them know that I care about them and their future.* I then went over and slapped my hand down hard on the desks of the two sleeping ones, smiled, and said firmly, "You will *not* sleep through this class, or your life, while I am here." They reluctantly sat up straighter, but they did sit up.

One of the first exercises we did was the Path Elements Profile, and we asked the students to identify which elements they were. Twelve of them were Wind or Fire, four were Water, and one was Earth.

Now that right there says a lot about the group's composition. Winds and Fires are usually the ones who are going to stir up mischief or break the rules to get attention, and they are also least likely to do well in an academic setting that is based on Earth principles. So, it was no surprise when I asked them, "Who are you?" and there was only silence in the room.

Finally one mumbled, "A student." Another one in the far corner mumbled, "A dropout."

I then asked them what their greatest fears were. Again, silence. Finally "Mark," a seventeen-year-old in the back, said, "I don't think I'm going to graduate."

In the next six hours we proceeded to download all the negative prophecies they had been given, and we turned them into positive prophecies that they repeated out loud to one another. We asked them to draw their "talent shields," showing their four most cherished gifts. We also had them write a mission statement for their lives, using the formula I developed and have written about in *The Path*.

I used the last forty-five minutes of the class to have them draft their vision statements for their lives, using the exercise I related earlier in this chapter. Now, you might think that a group of first-offender juvies who've been saddled with a boatload of negative predictions would have no visions. If so, you would be wrong.

Mark read his with enthusiasm: "I have nine muscle cars that I own. I am always at the racetrack. I can hear the roar of the crowd and feel the sun hitting my shoulders as I reach into the pit to help with one of the engines." (They got extra candy for including descriptive details.) Mark smiled as he recounted his racetrack life.

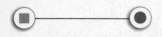

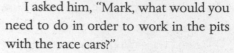

I asked him, "Mark, what would you need to do in order to work in the pits with the race cars?"

He said, "I would need to get certified as a mechanic."

I asked him, "Well, would you like to do that?"

He thought for a moment and said, "You know what? I think I'd rather *design* the engines that go into the cars than work on them."

I asked then, "And what would you need to do in order to accomplish that?"

He said, "I think it is called a mechanical engineer."

YOU COULD HAVE HEARD A PIN DROP IN THE ROOM AS THIS FORMER POTENTIAL DROPOUT HAD JUST IDENTIFIED A VISION THAT EXCITED HIM, AND A PROFESSIONAL CAREER THAT COULD TAKE HIM THERE.

You could have heard a pin drop in the room as this former potential dropout had just identified a vision that excited him, and a professional career that could take him there.

As he walked out of the room, he stopped to shake my hand. I asked, "Are you going to do it, Mark?" He looked me straight in the eyes and said, "Yes, I think I am."

It is no wonder that he, as a Wind/Fire, loves car races. He will now need some Earth component in order to get him there in a positive and fulfilling way. He could also use a mentor, which is another story in itself.

I share this story about Mark because it illustrates an important point for all of us. A vision, which is in alignment with your hard wiring, can be the compelling force that leads you to get the skill sets needed for a positive and fulfilling career.

Having a job is definitely a key component of having a positive future, but having a compelling vision is the force that will lead you to jobs that mean something to you and thus are compelling enough for you to overcome any obstacles that might come between you and your vision.

Of the 70 percent of people in the *Arizona Republic* survey who said they would give up more money for happier work, my bet is that 90 percent of those 70 percent are waiting for someone to come along and show them what that job is and offer it to them.

The world doesn't usually work that way. That is why it is each person's responsibility to seek and find and create work that is meaningful and fulfilling. I believe that writing down your vision and knowing your elementary makeup is a *major* factor in your happiness/career match. It can also help you advance in your career.

CAREER PLANNING AS A TOOL TO KEEP EMPLOYEES LOYAL

Wise team leaders are now incorporating career planning into their recruitment and retention plans for personnel. According to a recent survey, more than 38 percent of major companies are either offering or contemplating offering career planning as a recruitment and retention tool. At one time people were just glad to have a job, but current research shows that most people today have a choice of where they work and why.

According to one article I read, management needs to look at each person on the team as a "volunteer." Even if employees are getting paid, every day they have a choice about whether to show up on your team or not. The old days of hooking people into a harness and whipping them until they got you where you want to go are over. (One of my favorite Gary Larson cartoons shows a galley slave holding up his hand and calling out to the formidable man with a whip in front of them: "Yoo-hoo! I think I am getting a blister!")

Another survey stated that 50 percent of all people at work today are actively thinking about or planning their next career move.

Therefore, it would be wise for team leaders to intercept that process in a positive way by helping team members identify their areas of greatest strength and interests within the team construct rather than waiting until they give notice that they are leaving. Understanding the elementary makeup of each person on the team is a profound way to help them make their career moves, within or without the organization.

AVOID MISMATCHES

An example I have often used in my seminars is that of a personal friend whom I shall call "Susan." For the ten years I have known her, Susan has always wanted to be a middle school principal. While she was working on her master's degree, she was teaching in a local school and designed a program for gifted students. Her work in that field became so well known that leaders up the ladder decided they could use her to disseminate the program information throughout the state. They came to her with this offer: "Susan, we have gotten a grant that would allow you to travel throughout the state and teach other schools about your program for gifted students."

When Susan asked for further details, they revealed that she would have to suspend her current schooling, but she would get to travel three weeks out of every month. The program was funded for one year only, but it paid ten thousand dollars more than her current job.

Susan called me—and a number of other friends—and asked me if I thought she should take the job. I offered to help her determine her Path Elements Profile, and it turned out she was a total Earth. I therefore advised her not to take the job, but to remain on her predetermined path toward the principal's position at the middle school.

All of her other friends, without exception, told her to take the job. Why?

My guess is that they looked only at the money. Ten thousand dollars a year is a significant and instant pay increase for any teacher. Yet if you've been following me on the importance of the elements, you would probably agree that the job they were outlining would be a misery maker for someone who thrives on order, routine, and security. Funding for only one year? She would be losing sleep at night. A different town every week? She would develop an ulcer in no time.

However, this type of job would be heaven for someone whose Path Elements Profile is a Wind. Funding for only one year? A Wind would say, "So what? I'll figure out something when the time comes." A different town every week? A Wind would say, "Yipppeee! Where do I sign up?"

It is vitally important for team leaders, and for individuals, to seek and find a career path that matches up with, or is in full alignment with, each individual's elementary makeup.

Who Not to Hire to Take a Census

I was listening to the highly successful *Beth and Bill Show*, which airs weekday mornings in the Phoenix market. These two radio hosts are hilarious, spontaneous and engaging. One reason they have continued to be successful is that one never knows what Beth or Bill is going to say. This particular morning Beth was laughing about the time she and her sister were hired to do the 1980 census in a small town in Indiana. Turns out, according to Beth, the entire census had to be redone.

She and her sister decided to estimate household members based on the number of cars in the driveway and round up their estimates to the next best guess. When their boss learned of their methodology, the entire census had to be redone. Bill was laughing hysterically, as was I in the car, because that job was so obviously not in line with who Beth is. As you might guess, anyone who is on a radio talk show is probably a Wind, not an Earth, and an Earth personality type is definitely someone you would want in any endeavor where numbers are involved. How Beth McDonald found her way from census taking in the 1980s to entertaining hundreds of thousands of listeners every morning in Phoenix is a story I am sure is worth the telling. I, for one, am glad she did because she makes me laugh every morning as I am preparing for my day.

Shedding What Doesn't Suit Her

Another friend of mine, Susanna, writes character and leadership development material for high schools. She has been doing this successfully for more than thirty years. At one point she was actually part owner of a publishing company that published this material, but she found the work of administration and management very draining. Eventually she sold off all parts of the company that did not require her (or allow her) to use her highest gift, which is writing. She also lives in a community where there are potluck dinners virtually every night in the summer and fall, and she and her husband delight in mingling with their neighbors at these events. Recently I asked Susanna to do a PEP assessment, and it turns out, not surprisingly, that she is a Water/Wind.

This explains her love of helping people and needing free time to engage with them, as well as her dislike of the administration portion of the business. She was wise enough to shed what did not suit her and keep the part of the company that did.

The Lawyer Who Just Wanted Everyone to Get Along

Steve was a frustrated attorney. He admitted to me one day that he hated the confrontational aspects of his work. He thought about leaving the profession, but his income was so high, and his family's expectations were so intense, that he felt trapped. We did some career counseling and explored areas of law that were not so confrontational, but could actually be healing. He left the divorce court and became a mediator. He also gave up his home office and moved into a small firm where he could interact with others in a positive way. As you may have guessed, Jim was a Wind/Water living the mismatched life of an Earth/Fire.

Knowing who you are, and what your elementary disposition is, can determine whether your career offers you bliss or misery.

After my first book, *Jesus, CEO: Using Ancient Wisdom for Visionary Leadership*, was published, I was invited to speak to business leaders in many fascinating locations. Perhaps the most spectacular was a palace in Vienna, Austria, where I addressed 250 corporate and business leaders. As I looked out over the sea of faces, I asked them this question: "What percentage of people would you say are in the wrong jobs?" The answer was 75 percent. I was stunned, as were they, at their response. When I ask American corporate executives that question, the answer is even higher. Typically Americans respond that 80 percent are in the wrong job.

Recently the Gallup Organization surveyed one million workers in 110 countries and asked them, "What percentage of time do you get to use your greatest strength at work?" Eight out of ten respondents said, "Never."

RECENTLY THE GALLUP ORGANIZATION SURVEYED ONE MILLION WORKERS IN 110 COUNTRIES AND ASKED THEM, "WHAT PERCENTAGE OF TIME DO YOU GET TO USE YOUR GREATEST STRENGTH AT WORK?" EIGHT OUT OF TEN RESPONDENTS SAID, "NEVER."

Think with me for a moment about the waste of time, talent, energy, and intellect this information conveys. If you had a car that was geared to hit on eight cylinders, and only two of them were firing, would you be getting all the power the engine was designed for? Of course not. Yet the statistics convey that there is an untold amount of talent that is unused in corporate America today. And if you consider how many people are in the wrong job, period, the waste becomes staggering.

I often ask my seminar groups, "Who can name a wrong musical note?" People think for a moment, and someone might make a joke like "any note I sing," but the truth is, as we all eventually agree, there is no such thing as a "wrong musical note."

Yet every one of us has experienced disharmony in the workplace, have we not? I believe at least part of the reason is that we have perfectly healthy notes in the wrong places.

And what do we do when the misplaced note identifies itself in the only way it can? We usually start yelling at the note: "Why can't you be a B-flat? We hired you to be a B-flat." And the poor F-sharp note is thinking, *I'm trying to be B-flat, but it isn't easy.*

I strongly believe that a team leader's first and perhaps most important task is to make sure all of the notes are in the right places.

Understanding the natural element of each person is an easy way to determine if there is a good fit.

Since my organization's mission is to transform lives and livelihoods, I have given the "livelihood" portion of the equation much thought and energy. As more and more fifty-year-olds come to my Path seminars to be trained, wanting to be able to define their life's direction, my colleagues and I are seeking to take our material to younger and younger people.

Research that I did for my second book, *The Path*, indicated to me that a great many children have an idea of what they were sent here to do, but we as adults proceed to hammer it out of them—often shaping them into the image of the unlived life we did not achieve.

One college chaplain who works at a prestigious medical college told me, "Laurie Beth, I can declare right now that fully 30 percent of the students in this medical school don't want to be here. But they are so much in debt, and their parents are so much in debt, that they feel trapped." Other college chaplains around the table nodded their agreement. "Many students are enrolled in programs they have no real interest in," said another.

I was reminded of the sad story I encountered one day on my break from speaking at a major university. The student newspaper reported that there had been nine student suicides that semester. Not one. Not two. Not even three. *Nine.* One young student stood in front of a train. Another hung himself outside his dorm room window.

Now, I have had a suicide in my extended family, so I know that there are many contributing factors—chemicals, depression, and so on. However, all other things being equal, the overarching message of a suicide is, "I don't want to be here, and I see no other way out."

These suicides by young people have energized me even more to try to work with others to show them how they can use their gifts to achieve a positive future.

As parents and adults, we may expect that college will help kids figure out their paths in life. Yet look at those statistics: Of the students who enter college, fully half will never complete it. Of those who do, fewer than one-third will enter careers they received their degrees in, while another third will return home upon graduation and live with their parents for another year while they try to figure it out.

Okay, so college isn't exactly helping them all. How about high school? Well, in Arizona, where I currently reside, three out of ten students do not complete high school. Of those who do, only half proceed to college.

Career counselors—those who are supposed to help kids figure out their places in life—are swamped. The latest statistic I read was that the ratio of career counselors to students in Arizona is 1 per 750 students. How much positive, thoughtful reflection does that allow the people trying to help students figure it out? Not much.

Let's look at another statistic. Currently there are more than thirty-seven thousand ways to make a living in America. The Internal Revenue Service lists more than four hundred tax categories for different industry segments, ranging from animal care to mining and manufacturing to service industries.

One of the absolute best ways to make a living is to start and run your own business. Businesses are allowed more than five hundred deductions under the IRS code. I was taught early on that no matter what I did in life, I already had a family member who is a partner. "Who is that?" you might ask. The answer, of course, is Uncle Sam.

BE A SPIRITRENEUR

I'm passionate about the possibility of people becoming *spiritreneurs*, which is a word I created. A spiritreneur is someone who is a) honoring God in his or her work, and b) making a living doing what they most love, all at the same time. There has never been a better time in history to be able to live your gifts, honor God, and make a living while doing so. Yet you will probably have to find or make your own way to do so, as have I and millions of other spiritreneurs. It is not easy, and not everyone who attempts to open a business succeeds. In fact, you are probably aware that 85 percent of all business start-ups fail within the first five years. So, the cup is half full and half empty—full of possibilities and also full of challenges and odds that are against you.

WHAT MIGHT GIVE YOU THE EDGE YOU NEED TO SEEK THE MOST FULFILLING CAREER PATH? I BELIEVE KNOWING YOUR ELEMENTAL MAKEUP IS ABSOLUTELY VITAL, AS IS KNOWING YOUR MISSION.

What might give you the edge you need to seek the most fulfilling career path? I believe knowing your elemental makeup is absolutely vital, as is knowing your mission. Some of the most rewarding work I do is helping adults—and now students—discover their elemental makeup and then learn how that aligns with their mission.

Recently I worked with a group of thirty-five leaders in the education industry. One man was a Wind, and his mission was "to bestow kindness." A woman was a Fire, and her mission was "to risk growth."

As one woman was leaving the workshop, she said, "It was amazing to see the physical congruence in the people when they got their elements and their missions. You could actually see it in their bodies. They sat up straighter, and a look of welcoming themselves home seemed to pass over their faces."

Michael Gerber in his seminal book *The E Myth* talks about the kind of energy that is required for people (probably high Wind and Fire) to start a company. However, he also addresses the fact that few entrepreneurs are able to take their businesses to the next required level of sustainability and growth, largely because they do not have the skill set required. I would add that they do not have the hard wiring required. Winds and Fires are great at starting something, but if it is going to be long lasting, it needs to be turned over to an Earth/Water group for governance and sustenance.

Some career choices, with their elemental blends, follow:

WATER

Popular occupations for Water people include those that allow them to:

- be team players in an environment of cooperation and respect
- solve problems in practical ways
- concentrate on one project at a time
- prepare thoroughly and in depth
- work autonomously under a loose or minimum system of rules and regulations
- focus energy on activities aligned with personal vision, value, or passion

Preferred careers may lie in the areas of:

- creative arts/crafts
- provision of direct health care
- sciences and technical support
- clerical support
- service careers

WATER/WIND

Popular occupations for Water/Wind people allow them to:

- be involved in successful team efforts with a variety of people and projects
- work in a flexible environment of freedom, friendly relaxation, and goodwill
- be involved in creative, innovative, and inspirational efforts to produce results that help others
- encourage others toward personal growth while developing strong interpersonal relationships

Such career opportunities might lie in the areas of:

- creative arts, journalism
- health care or social service occupations
- faith-based or service-oriented occupations
- organizational management
- education, counseling, or coaching
- technical jobs that require good people skills

WATER/EARTH

Popular occupations for Water/Earth people allow them to:

- function as team members utilizing established procedures in a stable environment toward common goals
- follow a predictable schedule to work on tasks requiring keen observation and attention to detail
- quietly influence decision making toward the end of improving processes
- accomplish well-defined activities with clear outcomes that benefit others
- establish order and efficiency in the operations of self and team members

Such career opportunities might lie in the areas of:

- health care professionals
- teaching, coaching
- social service, counseling
- legal support services
- business or customer relations
- sales and service positions
- clerical or secretarial support

WATER/FIRE

Popular occupations for Water/Fire allow them to:

- organize their own time
- produce creative and practical solutions to problems

- connect with other people and promote the development of others
- exercise conflict-management skills
- utilize their good communications skills

Such career opportunities might lie in the areas of:

- business and entrepreneurship
- political activities
- strategic planning and development activities
- creative endeavors
- marketing activities

WIND 〰️

Popular occupations for Wind people allow them to:

- be active and free to act spontaneously in a responsive environment
- "spread out" and be expansive, both physically and psychologically
- focus on short-term accomplishments
- work with a wide variety of people and situations
- exercise the ability to motivate others
- utilize a strong sense of aesthetics and design

Specific careers may lie in the areas of:

- entertainment, promotions, or public speaking
- sports-related occupations

- action- or service-oriented occupations
- health care
- public relations
- real estate or finance-related activities
- trade- or craft-related occupations

WIND/FIRE 〰〰

Popular occupations for Wind/Fire people allow them to:

- work with other energetic people in loosely structured environments
- function in highly charged situations where they can use their communication skills to achieve satisfactory outcomes
- enjoy a constantly changing landscape of situations that encourages spontaneous interaction with many people
- pursue personal interests or projects or take free time when primary assignments or responsibilities are finished
- enjoy tangible results, products, or services involving real hands-on situations and people

Specific careers may lie in the areas of:

- action- or physically oriented occupations
- entrepreneurial endeavors
- sales
- financial- or investment-related activities
- entertainment, promotions, or sports-related activities
- trades, hands-on work

WIND/EARTH

Popular occupations for Wind/Earth people allow them to:

- interact with people daily in a warm, friendly atmosphere
- play key roles in decision making and be free to express themselves
- work within a clearly defined structure with a well-defined hierarchy
- receive external support in the area of organization
- experience recognition and appreciation for their contributions
- share humanistic values with coworkers

Specific careers may lie in the areas of:

- education or health care
- social service or counseling
- public relations or managerial activities
- general service industries
- sales or personal service industries

WIND/WATER

Popular occupations for Wind/Water people allow them to:

- work in a democratic environment with a defined structure
- interact directly with clients in an active endeavor
- work under a loosely structured framework with few rules or restrictions

- consider the needs of others as they work to encourage cooperative effort and juggle a variety of activities
- express their personal sense of taste, style, and/or design
- use their energy and talent toward outcomes consistent with personal values
- enjoy a sense of purpose

Specific careers may lie in the areas of:

- service industries
- entertainment or action-oriented activities
- health care or educational settings
- public relations, marketing, or promotional endeavors
- crafts, creative arts, or technical activities

FIRE

Popular occupations for Fire people include those that allow them to:

- manage and supervise others to keep focus on long-term goals or the broader picture
- choose direction, engage in long-term strategy, or organize systems for results
- exercise innovation and be rewarded for results with public and monetary recognition
- share their knowledge and experience by teaching/mentoring others
- interact with a variety of other highly charged people
- apply their skills in a well-ordered environment with clear guidelines but few rules

Preferred careers may lie in the areas of:

- business as owner/manager
- health or education administration
- real estate
- financial planning
- legal occupations
- computer-related careers

FIRE/EARTH

Popular occupations for Fire/Earth people are similar to those of Fire but provide more opportunities for the individual to:

- have time to prepare and investigate
- have access to detailed data and statistics
- have the resources of a competent support staff
- function within a stable and solid environment

Specific careers may lie in the areas of:

- finance-related positions
- strategic planning
- research
- technology
- curriculum design
- health care professions
- engineering, architectural, or highly technical occupations
- creative arts

FIRE/WATER

Popular occupations for Fire/Water people allow them to:

- lead and influence people
- implement communication skills
- have time to prepare and process ideas
- express themselves

Specific careers may lie in the areas of:

- clergy
- teaching/coaching
- counseling and crisis intervention
- therapy
- public health services
- creative arts
- human resources or customer relations

FIRE/WIND

Popular occupations for Fire/Wind people allow them to:

- meet new people with opportunities for acting spontaneously and freely
- design products, create services, or find solutions focused on helping people
- indulge their curiosity and participate in adventurous activities
- express their imagination and enthusiasm in a supportive environment

Such career opportunities might lie in the areas of:

- publishing/writing
- composing
- theater or broadcast-related jobs
- marketing/public relations
- strategic planning
- teaching or counseling

EARTH

Popular occupations for Earth people include those that allow them to:

- work in an atmosphere of stability, order, and predictability with established procedures and guidelines and a clearly defined hierarchy of responsibility and reporting
- apply a logical and organized work style to technical and mechanical skills to achieve immediate, tangible results with clear, practical application
- systematically gather, organize, and analyze factual information and use deductive reasoning skills to solve problems
- carry responsibility, exercise control, and make decisions
- be evaluated upon clearly established criteria

Preferred careers may lie in the areas of:

- systems and business management
- health care occupations
- technical or legal occupations

- sales and service
- technology
- education

Earth/Water

Popular occupations for Earth/Water people are similar to those for Earth, but provide more opportunities to pursue or specialize in branches that allow them to:

- have more direct personal contact with hands-on activity
- work independently but within a team effort to accomplish practical and measurable results
- solve problems with direct, simple solutions
- observe and enjoy the results of their efforts

Preferred careers may lie in the areas of:

- service, teaching, or health care
- crafts, design, and artisan opportunities
- health care occupations with direct patient/client care
- science or technical pursuits that deal with facts and offer variety

Earth/Wind

Popular occupations for Earth/Wind people allow them to:

- work under few restrictions with the freedom to solve problems using common sense
- be part of the action with a variety of people and projects

- learn and master new skills, usually enjoying a hands-on approach
- interact with other people in an enthusiastic and fun environment with room for spontaneity and a collegial atmosphere of trust
- be involved with tasks or projects that are of immediate and visible practicality
- exercise their personal sense of creativity, design, or aesthetics

Preferred careers may lie in the areas of:

- education or social services
- health care
- entertainment or action-related pursuits
- business sales

EARTH/FIRE

Popular occupations for Earth/Fire people allow them to:

- use logic and reasoning to troubleshoot and solve problems as they occur
- establish their own priorities and work schedules for accomplishment
- participate in a spontaneous, lively environment where they can move indoors or outdoors or "all around the town" and experience fun and excitement and variety
- pursue personal interests or projects during downtime
- exercise professional or personal power and interact with other "powerhouses"

- create, design, or initiate projects but let them delegate the tedious tasks to others

Preferred careers may lie in the areas of:

- sales and service
- technology or physical sciences
- management positions in established institutions
- dentistry and medicine

Any element can succeed in almost any career field, as long as it "teams," or compensates for its challenges. The important point to glean from this chapter is a keen understanding of the atmosphere you need in order to thrive. For example, I know a Wind person who has kept the same job as a youth director for twenty years—largely because her boss has given her so much freedom to innovate and create change.

Make sure you are putting yourself into environments that compliment—not hinder—your strengths.

PART III

The 28-Day Challenge

In this section I am going to take you on a simple, yet radical journey. After years of research and personal observation, I have assembled hundreds of proven best practices from industries around the world into twenty-eight principles that can help you transform a team of donkeys into racehorses, a team of whiners into an engine of growth, a team of doubters into magicians. If you practice these principles with me, one day at a time, your workplace will be transformed. I guarantee it.

In my book *Teach Your Team to Fish,* I wrote about how Jesus used the four elements of Fire, Earth, Water, and Wind to work with His team. First, He excited them about the big picture. When He said, "Follow Me, and I will make you fishers of men" (Matt. 4:19). He was getting them excited about a radical transformation, not only in society, but also in themselves. Think Fire.

Second, He grounded them. Think Earth. He said, "If you follow Me, it will cost you everything. People may hate you and even kill you. Whatever they do to Me, they will do to you. I tell you all this now so that when adversity comes, you will remember" (my paraphrase of John 16:1). In doing this, He grounded them in the worst-case scenarios.

Then He transformed them. He said, "If you abide in Me, and My words abide in you, you will ask what you desire, and it shall be done for you" (John 15:7). He taught them through example to be more than they thought they could be. No one who encountered Jesus left as the same person. Whether it was the woman at the well or Pilate washing his hands of Him, Jesus made sure that He transformed everyone He encountered. Think Water.

And finally He released them. Think Wind. He said, "Go and tell everyone what you have seen and heard. Whatever you have seen Me do, you can do—and better" (my paraphrase of Matt. 28:19 and John 14:12). He set them free with their newfound knowledge and transformation to go out and change the world.

THE MODEL WORKS

This model will work for any organization. I have used this four-point tool to help various organizations and institutions quickly determine where their challenges lie. Is your challenge one of Fire (excitement), Earth (grounding), Water (transformation), or Wind (release)? The very best teams have a balance in each of these four areas.

One team, for example, realized that they were unable to retain volunteers. After huddling around the Four Elements Diagnostic Tool, they realized theirs was a problem of excitement. They were somehow unable to excite the volunteers long enough to stay. I have found that one elemental challenge is usually related to, or masking, an underlying, deeper elemental problem. In this case, with a little probing from me, the members of the team determined that they were unable to *excite* volunteers because they offered them no *transformation* in their work. This new insight led to a quick and comprehensive action plan around what they were *offering* volunteers rather than just what they were *asking* them to do.

Within each area I have condensed and identified seven key principles, and I have provided real-world examples of how these principles work and how you can put them into practice on your team. Let's do an assessment of your team.

28 Days to Transformation: A Diagnostic Tool

(Copyright © 2004 by Laurie Beth Jones)

Read each statement quickly, and then circle true or false.

Excitement: Fire
Getting Them Excited About the Big Picture

1. Every team member has a clear understanding of the vision of this organization. True or False

2. Team members understand and often express what makes this organization unique. True or False

3. Team members are clearly aware of this organization's strategic advantage. True or False

4. Team members responsible for implementation have direct input to strategic planning. True or False

5. Team members clearly understand their direct link to, and benefit from, the vision. True or False

6. Team members are actively recruited for core competencies that are clearly aligned with the organizational vision. True or False

7. Reward systems specifically recognize actions that lead toward the vision. True or False

Total average score for this section: _____True/_____False

Grounding: Earth
Helping Them Get Rooted Enough to Withstand Storms

8. Team members have been made fully aware of all potential obstacles, costs, and challenges that lie ahead. True or False

9. Team members understand their direct and individual accountability for the overall performance of the organization. True or False

10. Team members have clearly defined short-term goals that link directly to the vision. True or False

11. All short-term goals are measurable and reviewed weekly. True or False

12. A 360-degree feedback loop is in place that allows for fair and regular internal flows of communication. True or False

13. Team members hold themselves and each other to a clearly defined standard of behavior. True or False

14. Financial, technical, and human resources are adequately aligned throughout the organization to ensure both near and long-term growth. True or False

Total average score for this section: _____True/_____False

Transformation: Water
Nurturing Them into Their Highest Capable Selves

15. Management knows the personal mission and vision of each team member. True or False

16. Every team member has a personal developmental plan and a coach or mentor in place. True or False

17. Personal growth and development of all team members are top priorities and action items for management. True or False

18. Leaders and managers model organizational values on a daily basis. True or False

19. The team is constantly learning and improving itself through innovative ideas, structures, and technology. True or False

20. Research and development for new products and services are integrated into all departments. True or False

21. Team members adapt quickly to obstacles, always keeping the vision in mind. True or False

Total average score for this section: _____True/_____False

Release: Wind
Releasing Them to Do What They Have Been Trained to Do

22. Team members are aware of, and are operating out of, their highest strengths at least 85 percent of their time. True or False

23. Team members know they have clear authority to release company resources and services on behalf of customers, staff, and stakeholders. True or False

24. Team members leverage their core competencies through strategic alliances. True or False

25. Team members have fair and well-proportioned workloads that allow flexibility and freedom. True or False

26. Meetings are well planned, brief, and empowering. True or False

27. Roles and responsibilities are clearly defined. True or False

28. Each team member can "message" and demonstrate the organizational vision at any time, under any circumstances. True or False

Total average score for this section: _____True/_____False

Instructions

How does your team stack up?

Total all scores.

21 or more True: Excellent
16–20 True: Good
10–15 True: Needs improvement
Less than 10 True: Heading for disaster

Now take your scores for each section, and determine which of the four elements are your team's strong points or weaknesses.

For example, the fictional company Aceworks had these responses:

Fire: Excitement	4 True, 3 False
Earth: Grounding	3 True, 4 False
Water: Transformation	1 True, 6 False
Wind: Release	5 True, 2 False

The Aceworks team obviously is strongest in Wind (release), with 5 True and only 2 False. It is weakest in Water (transformation), as evidenced by its scores of 6 False and only 1 True.

CONCLUSION

Basically this team is actively releasing (strength) untransformed people (weakness), products, or services into the world, with the obvious results and challenges. (For a more comprehensive overview of your team, please contact us at www.lauriebethjones.com.)

When I did this diagnostic test with my team years ago, it revealed that we were actively releasing very excited people, but we were lacking the in grounding structures that would support transformed people. We've been working on that ever since. By diagnosing your team according to the elements, you too can quickly get an overview of your team's strengths and challenges.

In order to help you gain more balance among each of the four elements, I have assembled some real-life stories and solutions which might help you with your team in the section that follows.

7

ELEMENT ONE:
THE EXCITEMENT OF FIRE

Fire is all about excitement. Fire is also about focus—bringing disparate strands and sticks of strategy and turning them into fuel for the future. Jesus was able to recruit the working poor because He ignited the passion in them to make a difference. "You right now are fishing for food. Follow me and we will fish for men," He said (Matt. 4:19). "You think you came here for water. I am telling you that together we will find water that will well up to eternal life" (my paraphrase of John 4:14). He used rich metaphors and working class examples to get them to see the big picture of what He was asking them to do. And they followed Him.

Currently companies spend billions of dollars trying to excite and motivate employees. If your team has no fire, no zest, no zeal, or had it once and lost it, you can follow these seven steps to ignite passions:

Day 1. Make sure every team member has a clear understanding of the vision of your organization.

I have actually seen this principle most demonstrated in a church I visited on the East coast. The church driver sent to pick me up said in the course of our drive-time conversation, "you are going to love hearing the plans we have for this place." As we pulled into the parking lot he pointed to a spot and said "That is where we are going to put the new community center." I went inside, asked to be shown the ladies room, and found two eight-year-old girls rehearsing their lines for the weekend play. They joyfully informed me that they were doing a performance to raise money for the new Theatre Arts center "that is going to be right over there." They pointed to its exact envisioned location. The janitor, the caterer, and the sound man were all abuzz about the new vision that obviously had been very carefully conveyed to them all, and each person knew their part in it.

A Harris poll of twenty-thousand workers, conducted on behalf of the Franklin Covey organization, found that only 15 percent of those surveyed could identify the top three priorities of management. That probably means that more than eight out of ten workers have no idea what the vision of their organization is.

This basic premise of understanding is all too often overlooked as everyone moves into the busy work of making things happen, no matter what.

In most corporations the vision is fuzzy or tangled up in jargon like "increasing shareholder value." I remember consulting with a Fortune 50 company and being given carte blanche time to interview employees in the halls and at all levels within the headquarters. Only one in three could state the company's vision. When I asked the ones who could state the vision what they thought about when they repeated the words *increase shareholder value*, they finally admitted that to them it meant "making someone else rich off our hard work." That can hardly be motivating!

When I asked how the CEO communicated the vision of the organization to the employees, they reported that he sent a corporate-wide voice mail once a quarter. Stunned by the infrequency of the message, I was nevertheless curious about the message. The reply: "He reads us the current stock prices."

No wonder companies so often lose their way. Money is a short-term motivator of people, especially for new workers coming up through the ranks. (See Day 15 for more information on this.)

People want to be a part of something meaningful, something big, something that makes a difference. Make sure your team members see the big picture, and that it excites them enough to give their all.

My friend and CEO Doug Hawthorne regularly walks the halls visiting his 15,000 employees, randomly asking them to tell him the mission and vision of the organization, and their part in it.

I commented one time that I was amazed that he took so much time to do this. He smiled and said "This is actually the most important thing I do!"

Day 2. Ensure that team members understand and often express what makes your organization unique.

One way to make sure your team stays hot is to make sure each person is on fire with the same message. Author Ethan M. Rasiel writes in his book *The McKinsey Way* (McGraw Hill, 1999) that elevators can lift your team in more ways than one. He states, "Make sure that you and they know your solution (or product or business) so thoroughly that you can explain it clearly and precisely to your client (or customer or investor) in 30 seconds. If you can do that, then you understand what you're doing well enough to sell your solution."

Imagine you were on an elevator with someone, and you had to tell them in 30 seconds (the average elevator ride) what makes your company unique. Jason Klein instituted the elevator test when he took over as president of *Field & Stream* magazine. He stated, "My sales force could not explain the magazine to customers. Our advertisement space was shrinking. Then I trained my entire sales force on the elevator test. I challenged them to explain the magazine to me in 30 seconds. It became a valuable tool for them, and our ad base has grown every year."

Political consultants James Carville and Paul Begala offer pithy and wise advice in their *Business Week* best-selling book called *Buck Up, Suck Up . . . and Come Back When You Foul Up*. Using experience from their winning campaign strategies, they share hilarious and telling stories about their work with winners and losers on the campaign trail. Since they have become so good at what they do, they are often called in to "fix" an ailing campaign.

They share that as they walk through the headquarters of the candidate's offices, they ask people, "What do you think is going wrong here?" Some people will say, "The color is different on the flyers from the one we are using on the street signs." Someone else will say, "People are putting up the signs in places that don't matter." Someone else will say, "We are not getting this information out fast enough." Finally they gather all the workers in a room, and invariably someone in the back will raise his hand and say, "I think the main problem here is, we aren't even sure as a team why they should vote for us and not them."

Carville says that unless everyone on the campaign team can state clearly the vision about why the candidate is the best choice, it doesn't matter whether the colors match on the signs or where the signs are or are not being placed.

Day 3. Educate team members clearly about your organization's strategic advantage.

Ioanna Morfessis was the founding President/CEO of the Greater Phoenix Economic Council (GPEC). GPEC's mission was to unify the business, government, and educational resources of the metropolitan Phoenix area to rebuild its economy and generate new jobs and private capital investment in the economy. I interviewed her for this book, and following are some excerpts.

> GPEC fused the economic development efforts of Maricopa County and fifteen of its cities and towns during one of the most difficult recessionary periods of the region's history. Most leaders agreed that something different needed to be done to counteract the serious impact of the recession.
>
> The strategic advantage of the Greater Phoenix region at that

time was its affordability, especially when compared to Southern California and other higher cost urban markets. Still other advantages included a workforce with outstanding work ethics; a pro-business governmental structure at the state and local levels; modern and well-developed infrastructure, especially Phoenix Sky Harbor Airport; and a diverse economy, including high tech manufacturing, professional services, finance, etc.

Virtually 100 percent of my time was spent communicating—coaching, advising, listening, soliciting opinions, etc. Many of our top corporate leaders were fabulous in their mentorship; often they would tell me "you have to tell them, and tell them, and tell them again." This was both internal to the organization as well as to its many external stakeholders, all of whom wanted results really fast.

Keeping the team on message required an enormous and genuine commitment. Coaching leaders in business, education, and government across fifteen different regions *to keep repeating the strategic advantages of Phoenix at every opportunity* was an exciting and rewarding challenge.

It worked. GPEC was able to attract such industry giants as Intel, Charles Schwab, and others, creating billions of dollars in economic impact in a region struggling to recover from an economic recession

The Phoenix team that Ioanna assembled was ultimately ranked as the best economic development organization in the U.S. and as one of the top ten in the world.

Another example of a company having a clear understanding of its vision is Wegman's, a grocery chain of sixty-six stores in the northeastern and mid-Atlantic states:

With a revenue growth of 9% in 2003, Wegman's differentiates themselves from competition with what they refer to as "telepathic levels of customer service." "How do we differentiate ourselves? If we can sell products that require knowledge in terms of how you use them, that's our strategy. Anything that requires knowledge and service gives us a reason to be." Knowledgeable employees are "something our competitors don't have and our customers couldn't get anywhere else," says president Danny Wegman. Just ask Carol Kent, manager of the 20-person cheese department in Pittsford, New York, who was sent to Italy three years ago to see how Parmesan is made. Breaking bread with the Italian families helped her appreciate that she was selling more than a piece of cheese, she was sharing a tradition.[1]

Author John C. Maxwell writes the following in *The 17 Indisputable Laws of Teamwork Workbook*:

When Abby Kohnstamm joined IBM as senior vice president of marketing, the structure was so fragmented that in the marketing department, employees weren't even sure who did what, and even with seventy ad agency partners worldwide the company was struggling with annual losses of 8 billion dollars. She believed that the company's products were strong enough, but that the entire IBM team *needed a single unifying theme* for the hardware, software, and services available to customers. With her guidance, the company adopted the concept of "e-business" which became the single focal point for the company. A senior vice president who has been with the company for 36 years says, "We all had enthusiasm for this wonderful campaign. It had an edge to it and portrayed the company in a much more modern light." The vice president of marketing communications says, "The campaign has galvanized employees. We're trying to get all those people to sing the same song, read from the same book," says Maureen McGuire, vice president of marketing communications. This strategy has transformed IBM from being perceived as a dinosaur "back to leader in the internet space without any real change in its lines of products or services . . . an astonishing achievement."[2]

Day 4. See that all team members responsible for implementation have direct input to strategic planning.

Japanese principles of team-based management are infused throughout the grocery chain Whole Foods. Writing in *Fast Company* magazine (July 2004), Charles Fishman explained that in Whole Foods corporate stores, and even in individual grocery departments within stores, such as seafood or produce, team members have a lot of say about what gets stocked, based on local products and local tastes. Regional managers design their own new stores rather than take blueprints from headquarters.[3]

Other studies have shown that companies can have employees participate in decisions that affect them by sharing the context and rationale for the decisions. Employees who participate fully in decision making—from framing, collecting information, generating alternatives, making recommendations, and implementing and acting on the decision—have an increased sense of control and commitment.

In hiring decisions, if employees screen a potential supervisor, they become more committed to the supervisor eventually hired. In product decisions, when employees can give opinions on product introductions, they are more committed to the new product. In relocations, if employees have a voice in the placement of a new plant or facility, they will be more committed. When employees discuss strategy, they become more committed to implementing it.

At Semco, manufacturer of specialized electronic components in Willimanatic, Connecticut, factory workers set their own quotas and schedules, help design the products they produce, and develop their own marketing plans. When the company decided to relocate a factory, the company closed for the day to take all its workers on a tour of three possible sites and let them vote on which site to develop.[4]

Day 5. Make sure that team members clearly understand their direct link to, and benefit from, the vision.

Obviously any corporate vision includes financial success. Yet how is that really measured in terms of each employee's performance?

In the November 2004 issue of *Inc.* magazine, a survey by World at Work and Hewitt Associates reported that 77 percent of employers link compensation to performance, up from 66 percent in 2001. *However, only 17 percent of employers state that their incentive programs were "very successful in helping boost financial performance."* This may be due to poorly designed incentive programs that do not link performance to individual contributions.

In the article "Paying for Performance," reporter Karen Kroll profiled an Austin transportation engineering firm that has helped devise a clear way to communicate expectations and rewards. At Transtec Group, which has ten employees, they know that they are being judged on the seven qualities of productivity and quality, loyalty, team building, creativity, management, ownership of job, and ownership of company. President Dan Rozyski says the goal is to get employees to behave like owners.

Each year, Rozyski distributes between 25 and 50 percent of profits to employees. Since he instituted the seven standard incentive measurements, sales and profits are up about 20 percent in the last three years. One engineer developed a new software tool, and an administrative assistant boosted her score by volunteering to save time for the engineers by preparing their Power Point presentations. The clearly defined expectations, linked directly to a reward, helped boost performance.

Companies are learning that sharing the economic gains of reaching targets helps employees stay motivated to reach increasingly difficult goals. PepsiCo has a program called Sharepower in which all employees, 500,000 workers in 195 countries, who work at least 1500 hours a year and have been with PepsiCo for one year are given stock in the company. Such gain sharing is not altruistic but increases employees' commitment. Pepsi employees try to please customers because they know the impact of customer service on future stock performance.[5]

Day 6. Establish hiring practices that ensure team members are actively recruited for core competencies that are clearly aligned with the organizational vision.

Nowhere is recruitment taken more seriously than at Microsoft, as reported in this article. The authors state:

> Microsoft Corp. is unusually thorough in its recruitment process, annually scanning the entire pool of 25,000 U.S. computer-science graduates in order to identify the 8,000 in whom it has an interest. After further screening, it targets 2,600 for on-campus interviews and invites just 800 of those to visit the company's Redmond, Washington, headquarters. Of them, 500 receive offers, and 400— the top 2% of that year's graduates—typically accept. Yet that massive college-recruiting effort provides less than 20% of the company's new people needs. To locate the rest, the company maintains a team of more than 300 recruiting experts whose full-time job is to locate the best and brightest in the industry. That strike force builds a relationship with literally thousands of the most capable systems designers, software engineers and program managers, often courting them for years. In the late 1990's, the effort resulted in more than 2,000 of the most talented people in the industry joining Microsoft annually.[6]

Some people might say that Jesus' recruiting effort was random and non-sensical. Others might say it was divinely inspired. Yet if one looks at Jesus' objective—which was to reach out to those who were hungry, sick, or thirsty for justice—it makes perfect sense that He would recruit fishermen, a physician, a tax collector, and even a prostitute.

Within that small group of seeming misfits, He assembled a team of people who knew the spiritual, financial, and emotional hunger of the people in each village intimately, and were thus able to recruit their friends.

Day 7. Set up reward systems that specifically recognize actions leading toward the vision.

David Novak is president and CEO of Yum! Brands, which owns the Kentucky Foods, Taco Bell, Pizza Hut, Long John Silver's, and A&W Root Beer brands. In fact, Yum! Brands is one of the largest food distributors in the world. At the November 18, 2004, Lead Like Jesus event, Ken Blanchard interviewed Novak and asked about how servant leadership is affecting his organization. Novak shared the story of going into China and instituting service awards for their management team. China has become one of the leading and fastest growing markets for the distributor, and Novak was thrilled to be able to give out awards. He said he presented a recognition award to Ying Ling, who was manager of one of their restaurants. She was so moved, she wept.

When he came back the next day and asked her to produce her award to show to one of the new investors, she said, "I cannot." When Novak asked why not, she put her head down and said, "I put it in my father's safety deposit box at the bank."

Novak explained, "The award I gave her was a crazy pair of talking teeth—a fun toylike thing we give out to keep people laughing. Yet it meant so much to her that it had become one of her family treasures." Clearly rewards are not often handed out in China. How rare are they in your organization? Yum's vision is to have each customer experience an interaction that makes the customers want to return. By handing out such a memorable award personally, CEO David Novak demonstrated the corporate offices commitment to the vision.

Drawing from the book *The Toyota Way*, we read Jeffrey Liker's comments:

One example of a splashy reward system developed by Toyota in the United States is the perfect attendance award used in all U.S.-based manufacturing facilities. Attendance is critical within Toyota, because associates are very skilled and part of a team, and staffing is lean. The perfect attendance system rewards perfect attendance—zero unexcused absences in a year. Those who make the perfect attendance club are invited to a big banquet held at a major convention center. About a dozen brand-new Toyota vehicles are paraded on stage. A lottery picks winners who drive home the vehicles with taxes and fees all fully paid. About 60% to 70% of Toyota associates get into the perfect attendance club—not a single day of missed work or lateness. The total cost of this one-night extravaganza to Toyota for getting thousands of associates to come to work on time every day is peanuts.

Toyota's assumption is that if you make teamwork the foundation of the company, individual performers will give their hearts and souls to make the company successful. Originally, the Toyota Production System was called the "respect for humanity system." . . . The Toyota Way is not about lavishing goodies on people whether they have earned them or not; it is about challenging and respecting employees at the same time.[7]

Jesus said, "Whoever gives you a cup of water to drink in My name . . . will by no means lose his reward" (Mark 9:41). In this simple sentence He was teaching the power of specific actions around the "Corporate Vision" of compassion and kindness, and promising a specific reward.

Review Questions for Fire: Exciting Your Team

- Which of the seven topics did you find most challenging?
- Which example of solutions most spoke to and excited you?
- What action steps are you taking today to make sure your team gets and stays excited?

8

ELEMENT TWO:
THE GROUNDING
OF EARTH

In this section you will learn how to help your team get rooted enough to withstand storms and setbacks. After Jesus excited His team about the vision of "fishing for men," He also said, "Times will be hard. It is going to cost you—perhaps everything." Jesus said, "I tell you all of this so that when trouble comes, you will not fall away" (my paraphrase of John 16:1–4).

Too many team leaders try to recruit with the benefits and tales of the glory, and then are shocked when team members bolt out the door at the first sign of adversity. Taking the extra time to make sure your team knows the cost . . . taking the right time to get the right "fit" for long journeys, can make all the difference.

I went to a store called Runner's Den located in midtown Phoenix, and I had to wait for a few moments while the salespeople took care of the customers in front of me. When it was my turn to try on shoes, the salesperson told me to stand barefoot and then walk back and forth across the floor as he studied the angle of my arches. He went back into the stockroom, pulled out five pairs of shoes, and had me try them on. The first pair fit like a glove, but the second pair looked more fashionable.

When I looked around for the mirror on the floor, he smiled and said, "We have no mirrors here." When I asked him why not, he said, "Your feet are too important to make shoe choices based on fashion statements. We strongly discourage that." With that, I bought the pair that really fit me and headed out the door.

Grounding is all about taking the time to find the proper fit, to look beyond "fashion statements" and establish processes and procedures that are going to ensure a long and happy fit for employees and managers.

Once you have whipped your team into a fiery frenzy of excitement, you must take the next immediate step of grounding them.

As the corporate environment becomes ever more fast paced and hectic, it came as no surprise to me to learn that one of the grounding techniques some teams are using is to bring in "drummers" to help everyone get in, and stay in, rhythm. Rather than the showy "hit all the drums and finish with the cymbals" routine that rock stars employ, these corporate drummers who perform at employee motivational events use very slow and methodical, booming drums to establish a sense of timing and teamwork.

Grounding has many layers to it, and we will explore some here. To me, grounding means that the team is aware of potential obstacles and is ready to overcome them. Rather than leading with the vision, and then leaving them there, team leaders who work with grounding principles know that teams who are prepared for the worst will not fall away should the worst indeed happen.

Day 8. Make sure that team members have been made fully aware of all potential obstacles, costs, and challenges that lie ahead.

Southwest CEO's Herb Kelleher has fashioned a corporate culture that has been able to sustain one of the most successful airlines in history. Detailing some of his thoughts on how to do this,

Kelleher lists several principles. One of them is "Focus upon the essence, not the peripheral." In other words, summarize that this is the issue that confronts us; this is how we are going to resolve it; and now tell me how we are going to overcome (not succumb to) any impediments that might frustrate our proposed resolution."

Another thing Kelleher states is that to have a grounded team, you must "Make sure that your organization is prepared for massive change. You must instill a culture that despises complacency." Hold regular managers' meetings to discuss possible forces that threaten your organization, and encourage rigorous debate. Make sure that this debate filters down into the organization."[1]

Unfortunately most companies don't realize that a suitcase of bills is unnecessary to keep the best people. But what *is* necessary is finding out what's important to employees and giving it to them when they've earned it.

The following questions will help you get started. For more, check out Bruce Tulgan's book *Winning the Talent Wars.*[2]

Do you reward results, or something else? Most companies claim to want achievement, yet their pay scales reward everything but . . . If you really want achievement, develop clear performance standards for every employee and then reward people for exceeding them.

Are people rewarded consistently and quickly? . . . Great bosses reward it ALWAYS . . . Give access to special training programs or that coveted closer parking space. Small "free" rewards given often can do more to keep people than one annual raise.

Do you give people control over their rewards and how they're calculated? If you want your rewards to be meaningful, involve employees in setting them.

Do you fight to get your people what they deserve? Whenever I talk about compensation to groups of bosses I hear the refrain, "But that's all I can do." Fight for more money for your people.

Stop offering counterfeit motivations to your people. Find the cash and other perks to keep them fired up.[3]

In an article in the *MIT Sloan Management Review* titled "Going Beyond Willpower to the Power of Volition," authors Sumantra Ghoshal and Heike Bruch found that while many "change programs" are initiated, fewer than one in ten get implemented. They believe it is due to management's failure to understand that difference between motivation and volition. They write:

New research into managerial action taking supports the distinction between motivation and volition. Project managers in the companies we studied—some large, such as Conoco Phillips and Lufthansa, and others small, such as Micro Mobility Systems—rarely followed through when the going got rough. Only 10% took purposeful action to implement goals. The rest, despite knowing what they needed to do, simply did not do it.

Why do motivated managers often fail to follow through? Because taking sustained action in the workplace requires more than motivation. It requires the deep commitment that comes from activating willpower.

Wise managers encourage people to confront their ambivalence, rather than avoid it. Executives seeking true commitment push people to ask, "What's the downside? Does it feel right? Do I really want it?" That way, managers engage their emotions, and emotions lead to deeper commitment. One of the hard questions asked to determine the difference between feel good "motivation" and going the distance no matter what "volition" is this one.

"What will happen if I DON'T do this?"

Forcing people to confront their ambivalence is a more difficult way of winning people over than offering rewards, and results in fewer projects. Yet when those projects are undertaken, after passing through various tough filters, they are followed through to completion.

Day 9. See that team members understand their direct and individual accountability for the overall performance of the organization.

A Harris poll of 20,000 workers, conducted on behalf of the Franklin Covey organization, found that only 15 percent of those surveyed could identify the top three priorities of management. Fewer than half claimed to understand how their job description contributed to the bottom line.[4]

One of the latest and most successful ways to improve the bottom line is known as open-book management—teaching employees how to understand the company's "numbers" and their role in improving performance. And one of the most successful practitioners of open-book management is SRC Corporation, an engine rebuilder in Springfield, Missouri.

> Do employees working under the open-book system of management really know so much more about their companies than workers at traditionally managed firms? At SRC they certainly do. When Bill Fotsch was working for the farm-machinery manufacturer Case Corporation, he flew to Missouri to visit SRC, one of Case's vendors. Fotsch had been told that SRC employees knew a lot about their business, so he decided to put it to the test.
>
> While on tour of the plant, Fotsch asked a worker if he knew the price of the crankshaft he was working on. Fotsch didn't expect the SRC employee to know the difference between the terms "cost" and "price," much less the actual price of the part. But to his surprise, the unruffled worker asked, "List price or dealer net?" He then proceeded to name both prices, as well as what it cost SRC to manufacture the crankshaft, and his part of that cost. According to Fotsch, he became a convert to SRC's open-book management program on the spot.[5]

The following employee knew how important his role is in determining the success of an organization. A janitor working at a Domino's Pizza supply distribution center took an off-hours call from a franchisee about to run out of pepperoni. The janitor grabbed the keys to a truck, threw in a box of pepperoni, and drove several hundred miles to make the delivery and keep the store open.[6]

Day 10. Ensure that all team members have clearly defined short-term goals that link directly to the vision.

Rudolph W. Giuliani argues in his book *Leadership* that "everyone should be held accountable, all of the time." Stating that people in government sometimes have an easier time of accountability than corporate leaders, who must quarterly show the results of their efforts, Giuliani proposed making his workers in the city government of New York highly accountable for one of the most unimaginable metrics—crime. When he took office, the crime statistics were horrendous. There were 9,000 to 10,000 felonies per week committed in New York City, and anywhere from 1,800 to 2,200 murders per year. He said, "I didn't want to tinker with the Police Department. I wanted to revolutionize it."[7]

The centerpiece of his efforts was a process called Compstat. With Compstat, crime statistics were collected and analyzed *every single day* to recognize patterns and potential trouble before it spread. Giuliani said, "We used that data to hold each borough command's feet to the fire." The Compstat reports were distributed department wide. Everyone from the mayor and the police commissioner could see whose numbers were improving and whose weren't. Doing that allowed successful precincts to be asked for advice, while those in need could be offered remedies.

Compstat allowed people to have accurate data for which to be held accountable. The results of the new accountability system were staggering and almost immediate. From 1993 to 1994, major felonies fell 12.3 percent, while murder and robbery fell 17.9 and 15.5 percent, respectively.

Giuliani said, "Compstat became the crown jewel of my administration's push for accountability. With this system, it was proved that results could be achieved, and excuses would no longer fly." Applying a similar system to New York's Children's Services proved equally successful. Giuliani asserted, "No matter what you are tracking, comparing results to previous indicators, then demanding improvement, is the best way to achieve anything. These account-ability measures lead not only to better accountability but also to better morale. As each agency becomes more efficient and more effective, people feel more positive. Everybody likes to play for a winning team."

GE uses the Six Sigma methods and practices, which help employees and teams clearly and readily see that their daily activi-ties link to the specific goals and priorities of the business. Having a clearer sense of their individual impact on the bottom line is ener-gizing and motivating for employees.

Day 11. Review and verify that all short-term goals are measurable and reviewed weekly.

Harkening back to the Compstat story of New York City, Giuliani writes, "*The New York Times* commented that the regular Compstat meetings are probably the most powerful control device ever devised for police." In 1996, Compstat won Harvard's Innovations in Government award.

The notion of busy police captains and city politicians gathering at the same time every week seemed to be an impossibility at first, or a nightmare. With every borough represented, every Thursday and Friday at 7:00 a.m., different representatives of the eight commands stood before their peers and defended the command's performance.

But Giuliani stated that soon people began to realize that if they had concerns, they wouldn't have to wait forever or begin a lengthy process through the bureaucracy to get to the mayor—they knew they would see him that week and could voice their concerns there.

In Stephen R. Coveys audiotape "The Four Disciplines of Execution," he states that research conducted by the Franklin Covey organization determined that having weekly, effective planning meetings around the organizations three most "Wildly Important Goals" was the single consistent determinant of success in execution. In other words, the most sure way to see that goals become actions is to organize around them on a weekly basis.

Day 12. Establish a 360-degree feedback loop that allows for fair and regular flows of communication from all levels within the organization.

According to the book *The Learning Brain* by Eric Jensen, research from noted brain expert Santiago Ramon y Cajal has emphasized that the brain needs feedback from its own activities for best learning and growth.[8] Considering that most leaders I know would love to have an organization or team that has "one mind," let's evaluate what we know about how the brain works and apply it to teamwork.

To make the best possible decisions, the brain needs a large number of circuits and connections. Called "phase relationships," these circuits tie together simultaneous stimuli. Brain researcher Win Wenger has coined the term *pole-bridging* to describe how the brain connects simultaneous information. When people talk deliberately, perceptively, and purposefully around problems, learning and thinking go up dramatically. Studies collected by Wenger have documented gains from one to three IQ points per hour of pole-bridging practice. Some have increased IQ up to forty points in fifty hours of work.

One could easily argue that using such feedback practices as a simple "well done" are indeed feedback loops that elevate overall intelligence and performance of the "team mind."

Most great thinkers like Leonardo da Vinci and Michelangelo have kept elaborate journals of their work for self-feedback. Being able to constantly and almost simultaneously assess problems causes the brain to rise to new levels of intelligence. (One wonders about the standard practice of a *yearly* performance review as a functional feedback tool.)

James Carville stated that he was amazed how even high achievers like George Stephanopolous would be motivated to go the extra mile for the campaign in order to get a gold star pasted on their foreheads at the end of the day. Napoleon used medals as tangible tokens of feedback for heroic actions, and once remarked that he was amazed what a soldier would do in order to earn a little piece of tin for his chest.

I overheard one man say in a seminar that his company made it part of the corporate culture to encourage people to double check details with one another. Rather than taking offense at the follow up, people began to appreciate having their team members check in with them for regular checkups and feedback.

This principle holds true even when there is bad news.

In an article in *MIT Sloan Management Review* titled "Preserving Employee Morale During Downsizing," authors Karen E. Mishra, Gretchen M. Spreitzer, and Aneil K. Mishra stated when workers have a premonition about a future plant closing, they are able to devise coping mechanisms that reduce stress. The information may help stakeholders arrive at their own conclusions about the industry or company situation and prepare themselves for potential layoffs.

The 1988 Warn Act requires that a company give employees sixty days of advance notice when closing a facility or laying off workers. While some companies think that advance notice will encourage employees to leave when they are still needed, studies have shown that employees notified in advance are more loyal and will delay starting a new position until the appropriate time.

Kimberly-Clark went further and announced all expected layoffs at once to prevent people from spending twelve months wondering what would happen. Advance notice helps employees feel in control so that they can better plan their futures. It also enhances their trust in the management's openness and willingness to share sensitive information.[9]

Day 13. See that team members hold themselves and each other to a clearly defined standard of behavior.

As we emerge from the post–Enron, Tyco, and WorldCom fraud fiascos where corporate culture seemed to state "anything goes," the concept of ethics has emerged from a topic of vague discussion into one of strict compliance. The new, warmly titled *Federal Sentencing Guidelines* contains more than 624 pages of legalese that instruct federal judges on how to punish organizations, large and small, guilty of such crimes as committing fraud, polluting, and cooking the books.

Inc. magazine reporter Darren Dahl recently boiled these 624 legal pages down to five things you can do right now to create an ethical culture at your company and satisfy the Feds:

1. Create a formal, written ethics policy.
2. Require managers and officers to monitor compliance.
3. Screen potential employees carefully before hiring.
4. Develop incentives to promote compliance.
5. Encourage employees to speak up when they encounter problems.[10]

Creating a culture of accountability will help the most in preventing problems from being hidden or team members being misled.

Toyota's system based on continuous flow and the *andon* system is ideal for powerful behavior modification. Feedback is very rapid. The best kind of negative feedback is impersonal and people find out how they are doing without a supervisor even telling them—by uncovering quality problems immediately. As for praise or reprimands from supervisors, the group leaders are right there on the floor in a perfect position to give immediate feedback to associates. In addition, they are trained to do it.

Implementing *andon*—Toyota's "fixed position line stop technology system" is a system that detects quality problems. However

Toyota insists that an *andon* system works only when you teach your employees the importance of bringing problems to the surface so they can be quickly solved.[11]

The military is known for building team accountability by holding entire teams responsible for the poorest behavior of the few. A young Marine recruit I know recently shared that he and his entire platoon had to stand at attention for two hours because two members of his group had gotten into a fight. He said, "You can bet that we never let one of our own misbehave like that again."

Day 14. Make sure that financial, technical, and human resources are clearly and adequately aligned throughout the organization to ensure both near and long-term growth.

See if you can identify the source of this business quote cited in *The Complete Idiot's Guide to Team Building*: "The way to achieve success is first to have a definite, clear, practical ideal—a goal, an objective. Second, have the necessary means to achieve your ends: wisdom, money, materials, methods. Third, adjust all your means to that end." (Answer: Aristotle)

In Toledo, Ohio, employees of the Dana Corporation, an automotive parts maker, can spend $500 per project to improve efficiencies without management approval. This alignment of resources results in "more than 80% of the improvements being made without the plant manager's even knowing about them in advance," notes Bob Nelson in *1001 Ways to Energize Employees*.[12]

"It's all right to aim high if you have plenty of ammunition." The ammunition Hawley R. Everhart is referring to is resources. Author John Maxwell asserts that it doesn't matter what kind of team you're on; the better resourced the team is, the fewer distractions the players will have as they work to achieve their goal. He makes the point that no team can make progress without the support of the appropriate equipment, facilities, funds, and so forth.

Jesus said bluntly, "No one begins a building before establishing its cost" (my paraphrase of Luke 14:28–30). Make sure you have the resources lined up in accordance with your vision.

Review Questions for Earth: Grounding Your Team

- Which of the seven principles discussed helped you the most?
- Which one challenged you the most?
- Which principle are you willing to take action on now?

9

ELEMENT THREE:
THE TRANSFORMATION
OF WATER

A good friend of mine is a pastor of a small community church. One of the members owns a bakery shop, and every Sunday he supplies a beautiful hand-baked loaf of bread for Communion. Jeff, the pastor, dutifully breaks the bread, and each parishioner comes up, takes a piece of it, and then dips it into the communion cup while Jeff reminds the person, "This is the blood of Christ, which was shed for thee."

One Sunday there was quite a bit of bread left over, so Jeff took it home and decided to share it with his family for dinner. As he and his wife took the loaf and broke it, they handed a piece to their three-and-a-half-year-old daughter, Amy. She took the bread in her hand, waited a moment, looked up at her father, and asked, "Where's the dip?" He and his wife broke into laughter at their daughter's assumption that there should be a communion cup of wine as "dip" for the bread. Through her exposure to constant ritual, this young team member was aware that something was missing at the table, even though she was not yet four years old.

Some religions teach the principle of transubstantiation, which is the belief that the bread and the wine actually become the body and the blood of Christ through the act of Communion. It is the idea that what you see before you actually becomes much more as you take it in your hands, receive, and believe.

My friend Lee Ellis and I recently had a discussion about the "miracle" of transubstantiation in brands. Through expectations and beliefs, some people believe brands may actually become more in the minds of the customers than the products being presented. Harley-Davidson motorcycles, for example, are really just rubber and steel. But when the brand is applied to the product, it represents and triggers a host of emotions for the buyers, ranging perhaps from rebellion against society to denial of middle age.

Teams must be "transubstantiated" in order to be effective.

Two plus two equals five is a longtime tenet of good team builders. Where does the additional element come from that takes a group of people and turns them into more than the sum of their parts?

I picked water as the element of transformation because it is in nature a solvent. Water added to almost any object shifts the essence of it—whether it is turning dry land into mud or turning fire into hissing ashes. Without water there would be few, if any, liquids. The human body is comprised of 90 percent water, and the planet itself is comprised mostly of the miraculous liquid. Each person is rocked in water in his or her mother's womb. We need it daily in order to survive, and we find it a healing and calming influence, as well as a place for recreation.

Teams that are given great excitement and grounding, but are not given enough "water," will never perform at their highest level.

What is the miracle of water that you can give your team?

How can you as a team leader take what is in your hands, receive it, bless it, and turn it into something that did not exist before?

Following are practical and proven steps that others have taken to make sure their team is not only excited and grounded but also transformed.

Day 15. Verify that management knows the personal mission and vision of each team member.

"Jim" was in a start-up mode. He already had three team members in place and was in the process of recruiting a marketing director. He had in mind a young woman named Margaret who had expressed interest in the company, and Jim was about to offer her the job. Having been trained in the importance of knowing the individual mission and vision of each team member, however, he decided to invite her to a corporate retreat with the rest of his team. The purpose of the retreat was merely to "get" the mission and vision of each team member, and there were no other expectations for the day.

When Margaret wrote her vision statement for where she would like to be five years from now, to her own astonishment, she saw herself running a preschool day care center for inner-city children. Realizing that Margaret's heart was not in marketing but in working with children, Jim reconsidered and never offered her the job with his company. However, the next Sunday when he was glancing through the classified ads, he came across an ad that said, "Day care center going out of business," and listed a phone number to call. Jim cut out the tiny ad and mailed it to Margaret, suggesting she check it out.

Margaret followed up with a phone call and discovered that the owners were moving out of state. They were willing to let her take over their lease and their equipment for a total of four thousand dollars. She promptly bought the lease and the equipment, and thirty days later was up and running her own preschool in the inner city.

Did Jim lose a marketing director? Or did the world gain a necessary preschool center? Margaret was so grateful for Jim's thoughtfulness, she offered free day care for his employees for a year, which turned out to be a huge incentive to the marketing director whom Jim eventually did hire.

It doesn't take much foresight to see what was saved for Jim by his investment in a one-day retreat for employees. While all others saw themselves in expanded roles for the company, Margaret saw her future in another capacity, and Jim not only honored but also nurtured that. Imagine what this world would be like if all employers were as gracious and as foresighted as Jim.

History was changed when another employer noticed that his employee had a personal vision that went beyond his current place of employment. Seeing that Nehemiah, his cupbearer, was sad, King Artaxerxes asked him why. Nehemiah gave him the reason: "the city, the place of my fathers' tombs, lies desolate" (Neh. 2:3). The king loved Nehemiah so much, he gave him an unlimited leave of absence to go and rebuild Jerusalem. Scholars and historians credit Nehemiah's rebuilding of the protective walls around Jerusalem as breathing life and heart into Judaism, and calling the people back to their sense of place and self at a critical time in history. I consider The Nehemiah story a must read for any person in management, as it is a bold and verified account of a single person getting clear about his mission, and changing the history of a nation because of it.

The article "A Study of Spirituality in the Workplace," which appeared in the *MIT Sloan Management Review*, revealed the following:

When asked what gave them the most meaning and purpose in their jobs, interviewees chose the following answers (ranked from first to seventh):

1. The ability to realize my full potential as a person.
2. Being associated with a good organization or an ethical organization.
3. Interesting work.
4. Making money.
5. Having good colleagues; serving humankind.
6. Service to future generations.
7. Service to my immediate community.

In previous studies as well, when people were asked directly, they did not list money as the most important thing about their jobs. Of course, this result depended on whether the person was employed and how well-paid he or she was. Nonetheless, beyond a certain threshold, pay ceases to be the most important, and higher needs prevail. The desire for "self-actualization," as Abraham Maslow called it, becomes paramount.[1]

Day 16. See to it that every team member has a personal developmental plan and a coach or mentor in place.

Why are M.B.A.'s worldwide more likely to seek employment at the global management-consulting firm McKinsey and Company before all others? Perhaps it is because of McKinsey's stated mission, which is: "To help our clients make distinctive, substantial and lasting improvements in their performance and to attract, develop, excite and retain exceptional people."

At McKinsey., every consultant receives a formal performance review from his or her office's partner group twice a year, with the individual's designated development director offering detailed feedback, counseling, and career advice. Developing and mentoring employees takes up about 15 to 20 percent of every managing partner's time. The engagement managers also provide the consultant with feedback, evaluation, and development advice after each of the four or five engagements that span a typical year's assignments.

During each engagement, the consultant also has dozens of additional one-on-one feedback and coaching sessions with the more senior people managing and directing the project. In total, each consultant receives scores of specific, detailed coaching sessions per year. The company maintains that its in-depth approach to development is one of the main reasons why people join McKinsey and why they stay.[2]

The book *What the Best CEOs Know* describes an episode concerning Jack Welch:

> During a trip to the United Kingdom in 1999, a GE manager told Jack Welch about a "reverse mentoring" program in which the youngest people in the organization taught the oldest how to use the Internet. "It was the best idea I ever heard," said Welch, who implemented the idea with his top 1000 managers within 2 weeks.
>
> The GE chairman made sure that he practiced what he preached, getting a mentor of his own. "We celebrate ideas," he later said, referring to his budding computer literacy. "We put them online."[3]

Managers of BP's newly decentralized operations compare experiences and share ideas. In recent years "peer assist" has been expanded into "peer challenge," in which peers not only review one another's goals and business plans, but the best performers are formally made responsible for improving the performance of the worst performers.[4]

Day 17. Verify that the personal growth and development of all team members are top priorities and action items for management.

Following are examples of some companies that demonstrate this principle.

> In an industry featuring high pressure and burnout as the norm, SAS Institute has created an island of common sense, putting its people first. SAS institute puts its people first. There is a free, on-site medical facility for employees and family members, a subsidized on-site day care facility, a gymnasium free to employees and their families, as well as subsidized restaurants and cafés.[5]

Writing in *Fast Company* magazine, Charles Fishman noted what one company was doing right in regard to team members:

Whole Foods has always been clear that customers, and their needs, are the number-one priority. Employees aren't far behind. Whole Foods has a liberal dress code, pays 100% of health insurance for full-time employees, and provides full-timers with 20 hours a year of paid time to do volunteer work.[6]

Another company that puts its people first is 3-Com:

> 3-Com has dedicated space in the corporate office for all the personal "errand" work that absorbs employee time. The company has leased space to a bank, a laundromat, a dry cleaner, shoeshine stand, car repair (in the employee garage), travel agency, and other services. As the employees use time before, during, and after work to accomplish errands more efficiently, they also have more time to focus on the business.[7]

Day 18. See that leaders and managers model organizational values on a daily basis.

In a recent PBS documentary about Wal-Mart, CEO Lee Scott was shown speaking at the Annual Stockholders Meeting. He was emphasizing the need to increase diversity among management and said that the new rule at Wal-Mart was that the number of applicants hired needed to reflect the number of applications received from women or minorities. He then said, "I am so committed to this principle that I have elected to have 15 percent of my bonus reduced if this does not happen." In other words, he was showing his personal commitment to the principle.

Being an animal lover and volunteer with various animal rescue agencies, I have a deep appreciation for the leaders at PETsMART, who refuse to sell purebred puppies or kittens. Believing that there is a shameful overabundance of homeless animals already, they decided early on to contribute precious space in their stores to help adopt unwanted animals rather than make a buck in the profitable sale of purebred animals. To date, they have helped in the adoption of almost two million homeless animals and contributed more than $31 million to various animal care organizations around the world.

Reporter Danielle Sacks researched an in-depth article called "It's Easy Being Green" for *Fast Company* magazine (August 2004). Beauty company Aveda president Dominique Nils Conseil is quoted in the article as saying, "What I find in the beauty industry is not very beautiful. It can't be beautiful if it is not also doing good."

Aveda is an organic cosmetics brand that has offered holistic salons and store experiences for the past twenty-six years. Founder Horst Rechelbacher, described as "an herbal zealot," first opened an Aveda salon in Minneapolis and later launched an entire plant-and-flower-based beauty line. Boldly declaring that "by changing the world of hairdressing, we could change the world," he determined to change the not-so-beautiful business of beauty products by becoming animal- and environmentally friendly.

In 1998 Aveda discontinued a line of perfume after learning that the Indian sandalwood oil used in it was untraceable. Concerned that the sandalwood might be being poached, and in the process "sacred trees" were being killed, the new president, Conseil, sought new lines that would not only be cleanly harvested, but would also improve a local community's biodiversity while providing it with a sustainable business model. A new source of sandalwood was found, and the perfume line is now flourishing. Conseil has subsequently implemented a checklist that ensures that all product ingredients aren't harmful to the environment or the indigenous communities from which they come.

Charles Fishman wrote about John Mackey, the CEO of Whole Foods, another leader who models organizational values: "Mackey is a persistently puzzling fellow: self-effacing, but with a hint that he senses his own legacy. During 2002, in the heart of the recession, he took four months off to hike the Appalachian Trail, fulfilling a longtime dream . . . Mackey believes we will shun factory farms that treat animals like products." He eats eggs from the hens on his

Texas farm because, as he says, "I know those chickens are happy. They live in chicken heaven."

In his book *Awakening the Corporate Soul*, my good friend and author John Izzo recalls this story from the life of Mahatma Gandhi. Once, a grandmother brought her grandson to Gandhi. The boy, it seemed, had an insatiable appetite for sugar that was threatening his health. "Please," she asked Gandhi, "tell him to stop eating sugar. He has so much respect for you. He will listen to what you say."

"Please go away and come back in four days," replied Gandhi. The woman and her grandson did as requested. On the fourth day they returned, and Gandhi looked into the boy's eyes. "Stop eating sugar. It will harm your body," he said.

After a short silence, the grandmother asked, "Sir, why did you ask us to wait four days before speaking to my grandson?"

"Madame," Gandhi replied, "four days ago I had not myself stopped eating sugar."[8]

Clearly, walking the talk is the key to transformation.

Day 19. Be able to prove that your team is constantly learning and improving itself through innovative ideas, structures, and technology.

In the article "Cultural Transformation at NUMMI," researchers detail the amazing turnaround that took place as a hybrid organization changed itself through innovative structuring and a new model of organizational culture. (I provide an elemental analysis of their approach at the end of this example.)

General Motors had shut the doors. The automotive assembly plant in Fremont, California, had been beset by low production numbers and constant conflict between union and management.

An "us versus them" mentality reigned as union leaders were constantly at war with management. Daily absenteeism usually soared to 20 percent, and there were frequent sick-outs, slowdowns, and wildcat strikes. Trash was strewn around the parking lots, and alcohol and drugs were freely available on the premises. No longer able to compete in the rapidly changing world economy

GM closed the plant and laid off the entire workforce in 1982. At the time of the plant's closing there were more than six thousand grievances backlogged in the system.

Toyota, however, wanted a foothold in the U.S. auto market, and after years of careful negotiation, GM and Toyota reopened the Fremont plant under the prophetic name "New United Motor Manufacturing (NUMMI)." One of the first things Toyota did was to insist on collapsing the myriad job classifications and abolishing seniority.

Taking the hard-baked and barren ground of a hostile, combative, hierarchical "Earth/Fire" organization, the leadership from Toyota was able to create a new and fertile culture using its more open and communicative management style (Wind and Water) to create change. Rather than seeking to place blame for problems, workers were taught to take the time to empower one another to fix the problem. Differences of opinion were accepted and valued. Managers and line workers were encouraged to eat lunch together and intermingle with one another. Individuals were made to see how the success of the individual was intimately tied to the success of the whole. Decision making became based on one criteria—data—eliminating power struggles and name-calling.

The Japanese initiated a "go slow" system, tolerating ambiguity and searching for consensus among team members. What emerged was a new culture of mutual respect and trust, and that became the common ground on which the new plant and processes were built.

The results? In the first year of operation under this new structure, workers posted a 98 percent average daily attendance rate. *Newsweek* magazine called NUMMI "a model of industrial tranquility." The *Wall Street Journal* reported that NUMMI "has managed to convert a crew of largely middle-aged, rabble rousing former GM workers into a crack force that is beating the bumpers off Big Three plants in efficiency and product quality."

As the success of the plant continued to take hold, Toyota began gradually recalling its management and technical team. However, the company did so "only after being assured that its key principles had been successfully diffused, and that the American management team had learned to manage the dynamic system." The then NUMMI president, Iwao Itoh, stated, "My greatest challenge is to make sure that both managers and team members truly internalize the concepts. That is the key to successful diffusion."[9] (Notice the Water words.)

In this particular instance, a Wind/Water approach of openness, humility, and mutual respect helped transform a barren Earth/Fire wasteland into a plant of "industrial tranquility." Leaders at the GM plant were open to totally renovating their structure, and their culture, in order to succeed.

According to an article in *Fast Company* magazine (August 2004), General Electric's Lighting Division has been struggling. Its rival Philips took away all of its business from The Home Depot, causing a 7 percent dip in its annual sales. Yet CEO Jeffrey Immelt is pushing the division to foster innovation, and doing so in amazing ways. One of the projects they are working on would actually make conventional light bulbs a thing of the past. Rather than having a light bulb within a plastic lamp, the plastic itself would light up. This kind of innovation, so radical because it is taking aim at its own products, comes about partly because scientists are trained not to look for products, but to solve industry needs.

Modeling themselves after Thomas Edison, they are trained to solve problems, like darkness, rather than seek to invent a new product (light bulbs). GE has a number of interesting rules for innovation. One of the most notable is "Bet on the industry, not the technology." Although few people can accurately predict when different and emerging technologies will take off, GE is betting on the industry itself in order to maintain its lead.

Day 20. Understand and prove that research and development for new products and services are integrated into all departments.

Can you name the fastest growing company in the world? I'll give you a clue. The first letter is *e*. If you guessed eBay, you would be correct. Since down-to-earth Meg Whitman arrived seven years ago as CEO, eBay has grown from $5.7 million in revenues to $3.2 billion. This makes eBay the fastest growing company in history—faster than Microsoft, Dell, or any other company during its first eight years of existence, according to *Fortune* magazine (October 18, 2004).

The company's concept was simple: Take an online trading platform, let sellers attract buyers, and buyers attract more sellers. One brash executive in an interview told Whitman, "A monkey could run this thing."

Sometimes the best way to innovate is to keep it simple. Although eBay is flush with cash and opportunity, Whitman believes that "many companies leave their core business too soon," and she has had the discipline to keep the platform sound and let the buyers and sellers do the innovating.

In other words, the entire management function of eBay is to coordinate and implement the research and development ideas of millions of customers

Through their trading platform, eBay has more than ten thousand developers who are regularly and diligently "listened to" in order to better meet customer needs.

Wanting more than to help customers "have a pretty face," Aveda is determined to make the face of its products be environmentally friendly, as well. So, not only are developers challenged with finding new products, but they also simultaneously must develop products that help eliminate waste and help sustain the environment.

Fast Company magazine (August 2004) reported that Aveda integrates its mission into research and development functions. Realizing that product packaging is particularly wasteful in the beauty business, management instructed its packaging and design team to reuse post-consumer recycled content (PCR) in its shampoo bottles from 45 to 80 percent. In some packages the content of reusable material is 100 percent. Aveda won a prestigious design award for its environmentally progressive lipstick tube, and the new design led to the saving of more than $1 million per year in costs. The goal of Aveda's president Dominique Nils Conseil is to have zero waste, and this goal cuts across every department.

Day 21. Show how team members can adapt quickly to obstacles, always keeping the vision in mind.

When management at the Tennant Company, a manufacturer of flow maintenance products and equipment in Minneapolis, Minnesota, decided the price tag of $100,000 to streamline a particular welding operation was too steep, a small group of welders decided to tackle the problem. They devised an overhead monorail system out of I-beams from a local junkyard for less than $2,000, saving more than $29,000 in production time and storage space.

At Amax coal mine in Gillette, Wyoming, the main operating face was close to running out of material. Consultants estimated that $24 million was needed to keep the operation in production. A company engineer pulled together a team of volunteers who met on Saturdays and developed a plan that cost only $4.8 million and worked "like a charm."[9]

In the mega hit television series *The Apprentice*, Donald Trump wannabes are given weekly challenges ranging from making money through dog washing to designing new campaign ads for Levi jeans. It is enlightening, entertaining, and informational, to watch how a group of competitive entrepreneurs are constantly having to adapt to change on an hourly basis . . . ranging from impending rain on a polo match to street locations for selling lemonade that are not the best.

In one of my favorite episodes, one team was matched against another in having to raise the most money through selling rides in pedicabs (small carts drawn by a human runner). One team went to work immediately, hawking rides for $15. The other team wasn't seen on the street for a while, but it was because they were planning. I will never forget the look on the face of the competition when Team B went pedaling by, sporting giant ad posters on the backs of their pedicabs. They figured out a way to make money not from the pedaling, but from the "pushing" of businesses through the ads. They found a creative way to add revenue that didn't add an ounce of exertion to the person pedaling the cab.

When people are energized around the vision of a company, they will be resourceful in finding ways to make it succeed. Most individuals use only ten percent of their brain, and most corporations are using only half of their talent base. By immersing people in the cause of the organization, leaders can transform them into adaptable, nimble, and quick-thinking performers who carry through when it seems the obstacles are overwhelming.

Review Questions for Water: Transforming Your Team

1. Which of the seven principles presented here did you find most helpful?

2. Which ones are you already doing?

3. Which ones do you need to implement immediately?

10

ELEMENT FOUR:
THE RELEASE OF WIND

These steps will help you release your team members to do what you've trained them to do (freeing you to use *your* highest gifts).

Day 22. Show how team members are aware of, and are operating out of, their highest strengths at least 85 percent of their time.

In the book *Now Discover Your Strengths*, authors Marcus Buckingham and Donald Clifton report that a survey of one million workers in 110 companies around the world were asked, "How often do you get to use your greatest strength at work?" Eight out of ten said, "Never." Imagine the loss of energy and waste of time, talent, and potential represented. Sometimes, finding employees' strengths requires hours of observation and hit-or-miss wins and losses. Sometimes, they can be discovered simply by asking.

A woman named Jacque was working with a friend of mine, Shelly, doing educational screenings. When my friend asked her to write out her mission and vision, we learned that in addition to working with children, Jacque had always yearned to be an editor and researcher. "Getting paid to read and research would be my idea of heaven," Jacque wrote in her vision statement, and two weeks later I secured her to do research and editing of this manuscript.

Even though there was nothing on her resume or in her background that showed she could do these tasks, her heart told her she could. Her organizational skills, educational background, and ability to take complex materials and make them simple proved to be of great benefit to me, saving me hours of work and moving the book forward at lightning speed. By taking the time to learn the individual mission and vision of her team, Shelly was able to enhance the learning and income opportunity for a first-class mind at no cost or loss to herself.

We are doing intensive work in the area of educating young people about their gifts, mission, and vision, working through the schools and certain YMCAs. I will never forget hearing from a young man who came up to me after the program and said, "You know, Ms. Jones, I have been in school for twelve years now and this is the first time anyone ever asked me something about me." Managers and educators alike have a tendency to push down and input information, without taking the requisite time to find out the strengths of each person on their team or in their class.

Plato said, "Knowledge acquired under compulsion retains no hold on the mind." If educators and managers can find out what excites their team or class members, and then link tasks to that interest, results would be astounding.

(For more information on our Path4Teens program check out my Web site at www.lauriebethjones.com.)

Day 23. Verify that team members know they have clear authority to release company resources and services on behalf of customers, staff, and stakeholders.

My friend Sheila took her four-year-old daughter to the opening of her new florist shop. She "assigned" Sydney to stay by the door, greet customers, and hand them gift coupons for their first purchase. Many surrounding businesses in the mall where the new florist shop was located had donated coupons to give to new customers as well, and Sydney was very well versed in all the gifts and benefits being handed out. My assignment was to assist Sydney in her role as new customer greeter.

When the first customer came through the door, Sydney enthusiastically handed out the pink, blue, and green coupons. The customer looked down at her offerings and said, "My, that is a lot of great things I get just for becoming a customer here." Sydney looked up at her, smiled a toothless grin, and said in a very adult voice, "Yes, it certainly is. And if you stand right here by the door, you also get free air." The customer looked over at me and winked, while Sydney went about wooing the next customer.

Somehow, Sheila had so excited and educated her daughter about what they were doing at the grand opening that the four-year-old knew she was empowered to excite the customers any way she could, even offering "free air."

Speaker and author Barbara Glanz shares a story about a young man named "Charles," who happened to hear her speak one day about the importance of knowing your mission. This young man happens to have Downs Syndrome, but it doesn't stop him. He determined that his mission and vision in life is to help brighten people's day.

After hearing her talk he went home and thought about it all night. He spoke with his father about it that morning, and they decided that one way Charles could do that was to share some of his favorite quotes. He was always collecting inspirational quotes, so his dad said, "Why not share some of those?" Together, they typed up a year's worth of inspiration quotes, ran them off in multiple copies, and cut them up into fortune-cookie sized little pieces of paper.

Charles then proceeded to hand them out to each of his customers, where he worked as a bag boy at a grocery store. Soon, Charlie's line was longer than anyone else's. People were willing to wait the extra five or so minutes so they could get one of Charlie's quotes.

Soon, the inspiration began to spill over. The people in the florist shop in the grocery store decided that rather than throw out the unpurchased flowers, they could turn them into corsages. They did so, and began giving them out to harried single moms who looked like they could use a lift. Soon, the butcher began pre-bagging bones for people's pets and giving them out without being asked.

It was only a matter of weeks before that simple grocery store was transformed, all because of one young man who got clear that he could make a difference right where he was. His employer had enabled him to release his resources on behalf of the customers, and the entire organization was lifted up as a result.

Nordstrom's empowers its associates to simply "use good judgment" in handling customers' needs, and team members at the Ritz Carlton are authorized to "do whatever it takes" to keep customers coming back.

Day 24. Ensure that team members leverage their core competencies through strategic alliances.

Scott Carson, head of Boeing's Connexion Division, had less than a year to install Connexion networks in 1,500 planes. All seemed smooth sailing, until the terrorist attack on New York City. Virtually all of Connexion's orders disappeared, and some were calling the once promising division "a distraction." Carson persisted, and despite huge obstacles, got the division back on track to success. The way he did it, working with people who had seemingly different agendas, was simple. He said, "The goal was to intertwine our destinies," and he did just that, forming strategic alliances with different division members to help bring the dream to reality. He made it his goal to help communicate to other divisions how they would benefit from their sister business unit's success.[1]

I believe that if teams saw other team members as strategic alliances, rather than potential turf challengers or competition, productivity would be improved.

The bipartisan commission created to study the implications of the 9/11 disaster came to many sad conclusions. Perhaps the saddest to me was that the information needed to perhaps prevent and avoid the attacks was already circulating through various government agencies, but it seems that lack of communication and some turf wars prevented them from working together to see the big picture—so dots were not connected until after the towers fell.

This phenomenon of turf is nothing new and is certainly not limited to power in Washington, D.C. It seems to be human nature to hang on to whatever bit of information makes us powerful and not share it. This desire not to form strategic alliances could also be rooted in fundamental personality differences.

For example, I was working with the leadership team of a very large company in the Midwest. We had gone through the PEP assessment for each team member, and I had asked them to group themselves according to the corresponding elements. I then asked the elements to write down what would make them deliver awe-inspiring performances. Their answers were revealing.

The Fires wanted "more control over deadlines."

The Earths wanted "more information in an orderly fashion."

The Winds wanted "more variety in their duties."

The Waters wanted "more time to reflect on and process information."

I then asked the other elements what their initial reaction would be to delivering on the requests.

I asked, "When the Fires said they wanted more control over deadlines, what was your first reaction?" In unison the other elements replied, "No way! That would be dangerous."

When I asked the other elements for their reaction to the Earths wanting more information delivered in an orderly fashion, the other elements responded, "That would bog us down!"

I said to them, "The Winds want more variety in their duties. What do you think about that, other elements?" Their response was, "They are flighty enough as it is!"

When I asked about the Waters' request for more time to reflect and internalize information, the other elements replied, "All they do is go back and forth anyway, caring about people's feelings. Why would we want to give them what they are asking for?"

I replied, "Because they are telling you that this is what would be required for them not to go to Tahiti, but to give awe-inspiring performances! What would happen to you as individuals if every team member delivered an awesome performance?"

The replies included: "We'd all look good," "We'd all benefit," "Our boss would be ecstatic," and "Maybe we could have less work to take home."

"Then why wouldn't you give these people what they are asking?" I continued. "Not one of these requests seems unreasonable, does it?"

The team members looked at each other and admitted that, with some hesitation about giving the Fires more control, all of the requests were reasonable.

I then had them divide into teams and work out the details of five simple ways they could give each other what they were asking. At the end of an hour, the group was beaming.

"This is so simple!" everyone said. "Why hadn't we thought of it before?"

Day 25. Conduct internal interviews to see that team members have fair and well-proportioned workloads that allow flexibility and freedom.

It has been said that a camel will carry 311 pounds of straw. But if you put 312 pounds of straw upon its back, it will simply lie down. Many mangers seem to try to get more and more people to carry more and more of the work load, often resulting in stress or burnout.

Indeed, the average American now works longer than any worker in any other modern nation, and puts in more hours than their grandparents did. Despite all the technology, or perhaps because of it, workloads in America have never been greater, leading many people to leave or quit their jobs.

An article titled "Intellectual Capital" revealed that 50 percent of managers did not think that they would stay with their company long enough to retire, not because of lack of opportunity but because of the enormous stress and high demands. Within this group 90 percent personally knew someone who had voluntarily left the company in the last six months because of the increased workload.

However, when a group member shared these issues with an executive, he was told that a job at the company was a good one, there were backups for anyone who did not want to work hard, and discussions of work-life balances were not useful for business results.[2]

This myopic version of "Take It or Leave It," combined with an old time management style that believes that workers are lined up for miles, eager to replace the "cog" in the wheel, are costing companies millions of dollars in employee burnout, retention, and recruitment costs for replacements.

A wise way to treat employees now is to see them as "volunteers" who choose to show up every day because they want to, not because they have to. Allowing employees direct ownership of the strategic planning to begin with can make all the difference in their commitment to the workloads, and their willingness to take it on.

In the Franklin Covey Harris poll survey quoted earlier, 80 percent of the twenty thousand workers surveyed said they had no passion or buy-in around corporate goals. Without a sense of ownership, even carrying a bottle of water can seem like a burden. When corporate leaders continue to heap goals and tasks on uncommitted workers, stress is a natural result.

Our brain is hardwired to be able to concentrate on only one thing at a time. Covey estimates that we can accomplish only two things at a time with excellence. If we add yet another task, the excellence quotient drops to 60 percent. Adding yet another drops that by another 30 percent.

That means that if a person is juggling four major goals, they are only performing at 30 percent of their capacity for each one.

The much-neglected task of management is filtering out the

nonessential work items to the few "wildly important ones," and helping free each individual to pursue only those.

Day 26. Ensure that meetings are well planned, brief, and empowering.

USA Today carried a report in their December 4, 2004, issue titled "Not Another Meeting!" The caption under the cartoon that accompanied the statistics read, "Many bemoan boring office pow-wow." The report went on to reveal that when it comes to attending office meetings, 23 percent would rather read the phone book, 25 percent would rather go to the dentist, 26 percent would rather research car insurance rates, 41 percent would rather wash the kitchen floor, and 54 percent would rather mow the lawn." This no doubt reflects the feelings of many of us who have had to sit through interminable meetings about nonessential items.

Meetings are essential. But they can be brief.

It is no surprise that a man who is the founder of an airline known for its fast turnarounds at the gate has a few words to say about quick meetings. In *What the Best CEOs Know,* Herb Kelleher of Southwest Airlines says the following:

> Reduce to the maximum extent possible, the number of permanent corporate committees. Use ad hoc groups to solve particular problems; include people on them who actually perform the functions involved (Customer Service Agents, Mechanics, etc.), and then dissolve those groups when the problem is solved.
>
> There is no "perfect knowledge," there is only good judgment. Don't waste an inordinate amount of time on analyzing, studying, discussing, and planning (i.e., avoiding the risk of making a decision). Set deadlines on decision making—"at this meeting, within two weeks, etc."
>
> Focud upon the essence, not the peripheral—e.g., this is the issue that confronts us; this is how we are going to resolve it; and now tell

me how we are going to overcome (not succumb to) any impediments that might frustrate our proposed resolution.[3]

Kelleher also suggests that one apply these test questions when making future decisions about raising an issue in a meeting:

- Is this topic/timing appropriate for the meeting?
- Is this a question that is relevant to the group and something that others would benefit from hearing?
- Is this something that is unlikely to offend an individual or subgroup?

If you can answer affirmatively to all questions, jump right in. If you answer no to one of these questions, consider the consequences and determine if there is a better forum in which to ask your question—or if there is a compelling reason for using the group setting to address an improper example, so that others can contribute and all can hear the same response.[4]

Day 27. Make sure that roles and responsibilities remain clearly defined.

The Complete Idiot's Guide to Team Building recommends, "For the team to function effectively, every job description should be reviewed periodically. If it no longer accurately reflects the work that's being done, revise it, or risk problems ahead."

John C. Maxwell, author of *The 17 Indisputable Laws of Teamwork Workbook,* writes:

The women of the U.S. women's soccer team, in their drive to an Olympic gold medal and the World Cup, provided an amazing demonstration of teamwork, each holding herself and the others to a clearly defined standard of behavior. Mia Hamm, in her book *Go for the Goal*, explains the pervading attitude of team championship this way: "Soccer is not an individual sport. I don't score all the goals, and the ones I do score are usually the product of a team effort. I don't keep the ball out of the back of the net on the other end of the field. I don't plan our game tactics. I don't wash our training gear . . . and I don't make our airline reservations. I am a member of a team, and I rely on the team. I defer to it and sacrifice for it, because the team, not the individual, is the ultimate champion."

In the chapter titled "The Law of Countability," Maxwell describes the excruciating attention to detail that was necessary to demolish and replace the old Omni Sports Arena with the new Philips Arena in Atlanta. The job needed to be done quickly, and because of the unique structure, the only demolition option was to blow it up. The Loizeaux family founded and own Controlled Demolition Incorporated, pioneers of the safe demolition of buildings using explosives. The Loizeauxs found themselves confronting a situation where one mistake could seriously damage three other major businesses: the World Congress Center (convention services), the CNN Center (cable and radio programming with twenty-four-hour broadcasting), and a MARTA station (Atlanta's mass-transit rail system).

In order to blow up a building safely, everything has to go right, and every individual must perform every task to specific perfection, whether it is analyzing the building, planning the demolition, transporting the explosives, rigging the devices, or preparing the building for the safety of the surroundings. If one team member errs in the execution of his role or responsibility (even to a tiny fraction of a second in timing), many people and much property are in danger. For this project the cantilevered roof needed to fall straight down, then three of the walls would need to fall inward, and then the fourth wall outward. The Loizeaux family accomplished this feat on July 26, 1997, and safely brought down that structure in ten seconds.

Great teamwork is choreographed as intricately as any dance. In the case illustrated above, each person knowing his or her role was a life or death knowledge of "roles and responsibilities."

Day 28. Test to see that each team member can "message" and demonstrate the organizational vision at any time, under any circumstances.

S. Michael Joseph, CEO of Dacor Distinctive Appliances, claims his most powerful leadership secret is to orient the company to a higher purpose and to be consistent in following a moral compass. He further posits that "in a company that truly manages by its values, there is only one boss—the company values." A recent anonymous survey yielded a 96.6 percent acceptance of the company Value Statement:

To Honor God in All That We Do . . .
- By respecting others
- By doing good work
- By helping others
- By forgiving others
- By giving thanks
- By celebrating our lives

One reason each team member can "message" and demonstrate the organizational vision at any time is due to the simplicity of the core vision and the illustrative points.

Joseph goes on to illustrate that in the thirty-two years that he has been with Dacor, sales have increased from $50,000 to approaching $200 million. The company has nearly doubled in size since the inception of the Dacor Value Statement five years ago. The company Value Statement is communicated in all its activities, including the Web, business cards, and showrooms, and Joseph says that people have embraced it internally and externally.

At Estee Lauder, William Lauder advises other leaders to "clearly state the mission and objective of the company in a manner that gets everybody to understand and pull in that direction." He emphasizes the need for continual highlighting of the brand mission and statement to all employees and states that "as far as the customer is concerned, the consultant (at the department store cosmetic counter) *is* the brand, because she is the person who interacts with the consumer."

When I personally go into large office buildings I often ask the receptionist "what is the mission of this organization?" Invariably, he or she will point to a plaque down the hall and say, "It is over there." This is a waste of talent, because the mission and vision of the organization needs to be front and foremost on the minds, hearts, and tongues of every member on the team.

When you have that, you have "star power." When you lack that, you are limping along, held back by the weakest link in the chain.

Ultimately, the brand experience so eagerly strategized and fervently hoped for is determined not by the highly paid executives at the top, but by the front line person passing out the ketchup and fries. Failure to communicate excitement to them leads to failure to communicate excitement to the customer.

I remember so clearly being picked up in a limousine by a company whose slogan was "Legendary service." I was struck by how constantly every person along the "food chain" that I encountered was able to recite this to me, and do so with a smile and a unique flourish that showed they were adding their own touch to the process. The limo driver, the florist in the gift shop, the receptionist in the lobby, the elevator operator, the secretary at the front desk, and ultimately the CEO all demonstrated this vision to me. It was definitely a branded experience for me, and when I think of that company, the words "legendary service" come to mind.[5]

Ask Joan of Arc's soldiers what their mission was, and they would have responded as one man "Save France."

The Roman slaves that were caught in a rebellion against the cruel authorities had been inspired to sprint for freedom by one of their own—a man named Spartacus. When the Romans ultimately captured the small band, they said, "We will spare all of you—just show us the one who is Spartacus."

One man immediately stepped out into the circle and said, "I am Spartacus." Another one did the same. Then another and another. Soon, the entire group of three hundred slaves stood there, all under one name, one banner, one hope, one vision.

Their story has lasted for centuries.

Will yours?

Review Questions for Wind:
Releasing Your Team

- Are your employees empowered and enlightened enough to release a consistent message to others?

- If not, why not?

- Which of these seven principles most excite you? Challenge you?

- Which principle are you going to adapt for your situation, and when?

SECTION SUMMARY

In this final section I have offered four elemental categories for transforming your team. If, as a leader, you provide these four basics of the Excitement of Fire, the Grounding of Earth, the Transformation of Water, and the Release of Wind, you will have a team that will rise above and beyond its current level of performance.

If you take each of these twenty-eight principles, and review and implement one a day, I guarantee your team will be transformed.

In our time together we have learned the alphabet of each element type, understanding the basic needs and values of each of the sixteen possible combinations. We have learned how to apply this new understanding to everything from conflict resolution and team building to relationship enhancement and skills of persuasion. We have even learned how to use the Four Elements to filter problems into one of four basic categories, and apply antidotal balancing measures.

My vision is to transform lives and livelihoods, and my prayer is that every person we touch creates and owns fulfilling work and relationships.

I view the Four Elements to Success as a vital step in helping you do just that, and welcome your stories, insights, ideas, and feedback.

Blessings to you on your journey,

Laurie Beth Jones

NOTES

Introduction

1. Jeffrey A. Oxman, "The Hidden Leverage of Human Capital," *MIT Sloan Management Review*, vol. 43. no. 4, Summer 2002.

2. Ian I. Mitriff and Elizabeth A. Denton, "A Study of Spirituality in the Workplace," *MIT Sloan Management Review*, vol. 40, Summer 1999.

3. Jeffrey A. Oxman, "The Hidden Leverage of Human Capital."

4. "Hands On," *Inc.*, June 2004, 35.

Chapter 2

1. Peter F. Drucker, *The Daily Drucker* (HarperCollins 2003).

Chapter 3

1. Drucker, *The Daily Drucker*.

Chapter 4

1. Drucker, *The Daily Drucker*.

2. Lotte Bailyn, Joyce K. Fletcher, and Deborah Kolb, "Unexpected Connections: Considering Employees' Personal Lives Can Revitalize Your Business," *MIT Sloan Management Review*, vol. 38, no. 4.

Chapter 6

1. Glenn Van Ekeren, "Work," in *The Speaker's Sourcebook* (Prentice Hall Press, 1994), 56.

2. Ibid.

3. Ibid.

Chapter 7

1. John Izzo and Pamela Withers, *Values Shift* (Fair Winds Press, 2001).

2. John Maxwell, The *17 Indisputable Laws of Teamwork* (Nashville: Thomas Nelson, 2003).

3. Charles Fishman, "Management Whole Foods Style," *Fast Company,* July 2004, 76–78.

4. *Values Shift.*

5. Dave Ulrich, "Intellectual Capital = Competence x Commitment," *MIT Sloan Management Review,* vol. 39, no. 2, 24.

6. Christopher A. Bartlett and Sumantra Ghoshal, "Building Competitive Advantage Through People," *MIT Sloan Management Review* vol. 43, no. 2, Winter 2002, 37-38.

7. Jeffrey Liker, *The Toyota Way* (New York: McGraw Hill, 2004).

Chapter 8

1. Jeffrey A. Krames, *What the Best CEOs Know* (New York, McGraw-Hill, 2003).

2. Bruce Tulgan, *Winning the Talent Wars* (New York: W. W. Norton & Co., 2002).

3. Bob Rosner, "Motivate Your Employees with Financial Rewards," *WSJ.com Startup Journal, The Wall Street Journal Center for Entrepreneurs,* August 6, 2004, http://www.startupjournal.com/columnists/newventure/200407 30-nva.html.

4. Franklin Covey, *The Four Disciplines of Execution,* audiotape, www.franklincovey.com.

5. Bob Nelson, *1001 Ways to Energize Employees* (New York: Workman Publishing,1997), "Case Study: SRC Corporation Opens Its Books."

6. Ibid., 19.

7. Rudolph W. Giuliani, *Leadership* (New York: Hyperion, 2002), 71–75.

8. Eric Jensen, *The Learning Brain* (San Diego: The Brain Store, 1995), 145.

9. Karen E. Mishra, Gretchen M. Spreitzer, and Aneil K. Mishra, "Preserving Employee Morale During Downsizing," *MIT Sloan Management Review*, vol. 39, no. 2, Winter 1998, 84–92.

10. Darren Dahl, "Do the Right Thing—or Else," *Inc.*, November 2004, 48.

11. Jeffrey Liker, *The Toyota Way* (McGraw-Hill, 2003).

12. Bob Nelson, *1001 Ways to Energize Employees* (Workman Publishing, 1997).

Chapter 9

1. Mitroff and Denton, "A Study of Spirituality in the Workplace," 85.

2. Bartlett and Ghoshal, "Building Competitive Advantage Through People," 38, 41.

3. Jeffrey A. Krames, *What the Best CEOs Know*.

4. Bartlett and Ghoshal, "Building Competitive Advantage Through People," 36.

5. Ibid.

6. Charles Fishman, "Management Whole Foods Style," *Fast Company*, July 2004, 76–78.

7. John P. Izzo, Ph.D. and Pam Withers, *Awakening the Corporate Soul* (Vancouver, BC: Fair Winds Press, 2001).

8. John P. Izzo, *Awakening Corporate Soul*.

9. Wellford W. Wilms, Alan J. Hardcastle, and Deone M. Zell, "Cultural Transformation at NUMMI," *MIT Sloan Management Review*, vol. 36, no. 1, Fall 1994.

10. Bob Nelson, *1001 Ways to Energize Employees*, 97.

Chapter 10

1. Matthew Maier, "What Works," *Business 2.0*, December 2004, 58.

2. Dave Ulrich, "Intellectual Capital," *MIT Sloan Management Review*, vol. 39, no. 2, Winter 1998.

3. Jeffrey A. Krames, *What the Best CEOs Know*.

4. Deb Koen, "Compensation Questions Make Managers Uneasy," WSJ.com Career Journal Europe.com, The *Wall Street Journal* Executive Career Site, 6 August 2004.

5. Eric Yaverbaum, *Leadership Secrets of the World's Most Successful CEOs* (Dearborn, MI: Trade Publishing, USA, 2004), 43.

APPENDIX I

QUESTIONS
AND ANSWERS

Q. Will my personality change over time?

A. Traumatic life events may precipitate changes in personality
   in some individuals, but according to research conducted in
   1984 and then in 1994 by Costa & McCrae, the general
   pattern of an individual's personality traits is established
   fairly early in life, becoming more pronounced but not
   changing appreciably with age. (*Personality Concepts and
   Correlates,* by Lee Aiken).

Q. Are certain elements more common in one gender or
   another?

A. While historically and culturally men might be perceived as
   being more Wind and Fire (aggressive), and women
   culturally have been perceived as more Water and Earth
   (nurturing), gender has no bearing on individual PEP scores.

Q. What if I seem more like one element at work, and another one at home?

A. Anyone can modify behavior to suit a situation. In order to increase harmony and release more natural "energy" in a situation, it is best to consider what your natural element is—and is perhaps being forced to be. If you are a natural Fire being forced to act like an Earth, you may be prone to inappropriate outbursts and/or a buildup of resentments that can damage others over time.

APPENDIX II

THE PATH ELEMENTS PROFILE™ FOR LAURIE BETH JONES

Laurie Beth, your PEP is Wind/Fire.
The symbol for this is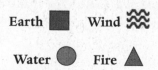

INTRODUCTION

Laurie Beth, this report presents elements of your behavioral profile. Before we get into the specifics concerning your own profile, here is an overview of the **Path Elements Profile™ (PEP)** and how it works.

There are four elements that determine profiles, and they are represented by the four symbols below. This report will help demonstrate how each of us contains all the elements, yet most particularly, one or two elements which dominate and drive our behaviors, attitudes, and actions.

Earth ■   Wind ≋

Water ●   Fire ▲

Earth tends to do particularly well in accomplishing tasks and getting results. Motivation is based on a desire for an orderly process that leads to accuracy. Likes to stay focused in order to "get it right." Tends to move slowly and is good at maintaining projects. An Earth's behavioral style reminds us of the traits of the earth: steady, predictable, foundational, solid, secure—"terra firma."

Water is sensitive to the needs of people and enjoys building lasting relationships in which it can play an encouraging and supportive role. Motivated by stability and harmony. Tends to move slowly like Earth and is typically good at maintaining. A Water's behavioral style reminds us of the traits of water: reflective, transparent, life-giving, easygoing, capable of "going with the flow."

Wind is also motivated by interaction with people but prefers a fast and changing pace. Initiators who enjoy networking with others in order to get things done and gain attention. Thrives in variety. A Wind's behavioral style reminds us of the traits of wind: restless, unpredictable, invisible, quick to move, needs to see things in motion.

Fire is motivated to undertake challenging tasks in order to get results. Seeks power and control in order to achieve its goals. Tends to move quickly and enjoy initiating projects. Fire's behavioral style reminds us of the traits of fire: hot, passionate, all-consuming, uncompromising, gives itself 110 percent to the task at hand.

Your **Path Elements Profile™ (PEP)** Report includes all four elements, and it is the blend of these elements that creates your behavioral profile. Understanding and utilizing this profile will revolutionize your understanding of who you are and help clarify why you do the things you do. It will help you focus on your strengths, as well as understand the challenges that have been hindering you—perhaps unnamed for years.

LAURIE BETH, SHOWN BELOW ARE YOUR SCORES FOR THE FOUR ELEMENTS:

Earth	Water
31	33

Wind	Fire
69	69

Laurie Beth, by comparing the bar graphs below, you can see that your strongest elements are Wind and Fire, which are both fast-paced influences. Like the wind, you prefer moving quickly and having a visible impact. You are exciting, spontaneous, and bring energy to events and situations. You tend to ignore boundaries, and people get swept up in your ideas. In your environment, you prefer fast action and immediate results. As Fire, you are capable of massive, sweeping action resulting in significant, widespread change. You are bold, direct, confident, and eager to be in charge of your destiny. To accomplish this, you seek choice and control of every situation, directing people and actions to obtain the desired result. Bottom-line results are important to you.

Wind/Fire draws from two elements: Wind focuses on what it can see and feel, moving forward at a fast pace. This element is friendly, talkative, outgoing, optimistic, and works well with others. Fire is motivated by overcoming obstacles and setting the pace to lofty goals. Takes risks, tends to see the big picture, and delegates the details that complete it.

The Wind element in Wind/Fire is enthusiastic, persuasive, inspiring, creative, outspoken, idealistic, trusting, and open to new ideas. Its Fire element is pioneering, visionary, and competitive, confronting problems head-on, and evaluating results, not intentions. The blended element of Wind/Fire is a motivator, persuader, and networker, coupling people skills with sharp focus.

In the next few pages, you will learn more about your nature and also the characteristics of the other elements and how you can work with and relate best to each of them. You will also discover how to draw from each of the four elements to enrich your life. Let's begin with your most essential element.

WIND: THE ESSENTIAL ELEMENT IN LAURIE BETH'S PATH ELEMENTS PROFILE™ (PEP)

Wind 69

Laurie Beth, your score above indicates that Wind is an essential element in your profile and is key to understanding your behaviors. Because of this, we can also expect that you will value and display most of the Wind-related talents in the list of strengths below. These will be key attributes for your success.

Keep in mind that there are also challenges that accompany these strengths. It is sometimes hard to see them in ourselves, and usually others recognize them before we do. When our strengths are out of control it's easy for them to be overused to the point that they become challenges. Also, these challenges often become most evident when we are physically tired or under stress. To achieve your highest potential, maximize your strengths and learn to recognize and manage your challenges.

Wind Strengths	Wind Challenges
optimistic	unrealistic
charming	manipulative
amusing	silly
spontaneous	impulsive
passionate	emotional
talkative	self-promoting
lively	hyper
persuasive	fast-talking

trusting	gullible
friendly	shallow
enthusiastic	loud/gushy
flexible	unfocused

Wind thrives on meeting new people, gaining recognition and approval, short-term goals, variety, freedom to express ideas, openness, activity, and time for fun. Wind dislikes being ignored, working alone, confining responsibilities and routines, paperwork, formality, and deceit.

Personal Coaching

Wind can be more successful if it will think before speaking—plan more, prepare earlier!

FIRE: A SUPPORTING ELEMENT IN LAURIE BETH'S PATH ELEMENTS PROFILE™ (PEP)

Fire 69

Laurie Beth, your score above indicates that Fire is a supporting essential element in your profile and is key to understanding your behaviors. Because of this, we can also expect that you will value and display most of the Fire-related talents in the list of strengths below. These will be key attributes for your success.

Keep in mind that there are also challenges that accompany these strengths. It is sometimes hard to see them in ourselves and usually others recognize them before we do. When our strengths are out of control it's easy for them to be overused to the point that they become challenges. Also, these challenges often become most evident when we are physically tired or under stress. To achieve your highest potential, maximize your strengths and learn to recognize and manage your challenges.

Fire Strengths	Fire Challenges
bold	impulsive
assertive	controlling
risk-taking	reckless
daring	defiant
results oriented	overcommits others
visionary	self-absorbed
direct	poor listener
confident	egotistical
decisive	opinionated
initiating	pushy
competitive	win at all costs
confronting	unapproachable

Fires appreciate and value opportunities for rapid advancement, rewards in keeping with risks, a variety of challenging assignments, and causes in which they can make a difference. Fire dislikes close supervision and doing ordinary repetitive tasks as well as indecisiveness, complacency, and excuses by others.

Personal Coaching

Fire can be more successful if it will slow down, learn to really listen, and consider others.

WATER: UNDERSTANDING A DIFFERENT ELEMENT

Water 33

Laurie Beth, your score above indicates that Water is a different element in your profile. It is likely that you do not rely on its strengths in meeting the demands of your environment. Likewise, the challenges that accompany Water probably do not concern you. Because you don't use these traits, you may not appreciate or even notice their value. However, Water has valuable characteristics and makes contributions that should not be overlooked.

While Water types may recognize their strengths, it is possible that others—particularly people like you, who are more influenced by one or more of the other elements—may notice their areas of challenge before they do. By valuing Water's strengths, you will see how many of their talents complement yours. Taking this balanced approach will improve your relationship with Water.

Water Strengths	Water Challenges
steady	complacent
satisfied	passive
team-oriented	dependent
good listener	closemouthed
loyal	possessive
supportive	used by others
sensitive	thin-skinned
traditional	lacks vision
cooperative	unassertive
quiet	timid
consistent	stubborn
trusting	naíve

Waters appreciate and value calmness, steadiness, clearly defined expectations, time for reflection, working at their own pace, sincerity, loyalty, and safety. Water dislikes insensitivity, conflict, inflexibility, lack of clarity, changing quickly, and being overlooked or taken for granted.

Personal Coaching
Water can be more successful if it will learn to say no, toughen up—and act now!

EARTH: UNDERSTANDING
A DIFFERENT ELEMENT

Earth 31

Laurie Beth, your score above indicates that Earth is a different element in your profile. It is likely that you do not rely on its strengths in meeting the demands of your environment. Likewise, the challenges that accompany Earth probably do not concern you. Because you don't use these traits, you may not appreciate or even notice their value. However, Earth has valuable characteristics and makes contributions that should not be overlooked.

While Earth types may recognize their strengths, it is possible that others—particularly people like you, who are more influenced by one or more of the other elements—may notice their areas of challenge before they do. By valuing Earth's strengths, you will see how many of their talents complement yours. Taking this balanced approach will improve your relationship with Earth.

Earth Strengths	Earth Challenges
accurate with details	picky
predictable	boring
reserved	distant
organized/scheduled	inflexible
conscientious	perfectionistic
cautious	suspicious
prepared	lacking confidence
analytical	obsessive
focused	unresponsive
factual	emotionless
realistic	pessimistic
modest	self-critical

Earth appreciates and values structure, stability, long-term thinking, information, quality, integrity, and commitment. Earth dislikes disorganization, instability, quick-fix thinking, inaccuracy, demonstrations of emotion, inferior work, and disloyalty.

Personal Coaching
> *Earth can be more successful if it will loosen up—and open up!*

AN IN-DEPTH LOOK AT LAURIE BETH'S WIND/FIRE PROFILE

It is important to understand that there are no "right" or "wrong," "good" or "bad" profiles. One is not better than another, although one may be more useful in a particular situation. For instance, if your job requires you to have a high amount of contact with people, you would probably enjoy it more as a **Wind** than you would as an **Earth**. This is because **Wind** is naturally more people-oriented and relationship driven. On the other hand, if you were involved in bookkeeping for your company, working alone on accounts and inventory, you would probably enjoy it more as a task-oriented, results-driven **Earth** than you would as a **Wind**.

In the same way, those who have a **Water** profile don't like making decisions under time pressures because they prefer to move more slowly and maintain stability. **Fire** people get "fired up" by that same time pressure because they are quick-moving initiators. Likewise, **Water** people tend to be comfortable when asked to cooperate with others in completing a team project, while **Fire** people quickly become bored and want to start a new assignment where they can be in charge.

Wherever you go, you are always adjusting your style to succeed, to have influence, to support a goal, or to be more productive. Sometimes, it is easy, because your profile fits the requirements of your environment, and you can use your element strengths. At other times, you are truly "out of your element" and must adapt your style to do what the situation demands.

This section shows how your Path Elements Profile™ tends to respond to a variety of situations.

Action

The Wind/Fire blend is highly spontaneous and quick to take action. Not particularly strategic in planning—just understands that it's easier to steer a rolling vehicle than a parked one. Fire's goal setting and vision supports Wind's enthusiasm and optimism, and both are high-energy. Can easily slip into overdrive because of zeal to achieve.

Adventure

The Wind/Fire blend embraces opportunities for adventure—every chance to "go and do" invites the unexpected. Fire asks questions about profitable activities, but if a challenge is connected to it, the activity will probably receive its endorsement. Both elements hate being bored.

Anger

The Wind/Fire blend is volatile and impatient. Both want immediate results. Wind tends to shrug off disappointment and look on the bright side after reacting emotionally. Fire enjoys "clearing the air," so there is little in the blend that would inhibit displays of temper. No interest in holding grudges; when it's over, it's over.

Authority

The Wind/Fire blend has little patience for laws and lawmakers that get between a goal and accomplishing it. Wind relies on its ability to talk its way out of anything, and Fire seldom looks back to see consequences of past actions. Overall, this blend would rather beg forgiveness than ask permission.

Change

The Wind/Fire blend loves change and may instigate change to escape boredom. Very good at motivating a group to action, but may become manipulative in the process. Lacks sensitivity to impact of change on others when excited about the possibilities.

Communication

The Wind/Fire blend creates a powerful set of communication skills that can be most effective in motivating and mobilizing people. Tends to be skimpy on facts and high on energy—a story-teller with a purpose can be very convincing. Communicates emotionally and can easily become manipulative.

Conflict

The Wind/Fire blend enjoys conflict that isn't of a personal nature. Fire's presence goes a long way in overcoming Wind's fear of personal rejection or social disapproval, providing boldness and confidence. Says things in passion that are regretted later—Wind and Fire can easily burn out of control.

Fears

The Wind/Fire blend's greatest fears are losing social approval and being used unfairly by others. Both elements have healthy egos—feel it is important to protect image and preserve options.

Fun

The Wind/Fire blend isn't interested in safe fun. Wind's impulsiveness and Fire's recklessness combine to create spontaneous fun—it needn't be planned ahead of time and may involve some type of team challenge. Wind adds humor and Fire adds bravado. The result is unpredictable and, if successful, creates an experience to talk about.

Ideal Work Environment

The Wind/Fire blend wants to do work that is "high-stakes play." Needs rewards and recognition for achievement and organizational assistance to handle details. Include when "visioning" new, challenging projects. Wants opportunities to "shine" and to develop important connections. Does not want to be ignored. Needs to see a future in continuing to work together or will go elsewhere.

Leadership

The Wind/Fire blend tends to look for an easygoing leader who allows workers to come and go, offers opportunity to develop new ideas, and provides challenging assignments. As a leader, Wind/Fire looks for similar followers. Verbally persuasive, affirming, action-oriented, with low supervision as long as results are produced.

Learning

The Wind/Fire blend learns through experience. Tends to assume it already knows until it discovers otherwise. May overestimate competence—often humility must come before learning. Optimistic about ability to learn and tends to be a quick study. Tends to retain bullet points and ignore what is considered to be useless information.

Leisure

The Wind/Fire blend's idea of leisure is activity. Wind's batteries are recharged by being with people, and Fire recharges through physical exercise. Does not like to be alone. Hobbies will not be passive. Enjoys listening to self-improvement albums and motivational books while on the go.

Order

The Wind/Fire blend is all about spontaneity, so even ordering the day's events in a calendar-planner is something that must be learned. Work space is typically cluttered with multiple projects in the works. Fire provides more priority and focus than Wind alone but still needs help in organizing materials, activities, and paperwork.

Pace

The Wind/Fire blend operates at a fast-driving, productive pace. High energy moves plans forward. Thrives on variety and the "thrill of the chase." Tends to overcommit time and underestimate resources.

Relationships

The Wind/Fire blend is people-oriented with influence from task-oriented Fire. Relationships may be based on agenda and productivity—may seem shallow to others with different element profiles. Friendships seem to be on compressed time—always headed off to somewhere else. Tends to run with like-minded promoters and motivators.

Stress

The Wind/Fire blend has a high tolerance for stress and handles time and deadline pressures as a fact of life. May express frustration and anger at loss of control with too few hours to get it all done. Often does not recognize stress because it has become so common. May have stress in personal relationships because of poor time management.

Success

The Wind/Fire blend views success in terms of personal acclaim, reputation, and recognition. Fruits of success are important and are reflected in lifestyle. Sometimes is content to "fake it till you make it," so may need help in translating talk into completed action.

Tasks

The Wind/Fire blend is primarily people-oriented, although supporting Fire factors focus on tasks and results. Typically an enthusiastic starter and not selective enough about which tasks are undertaken. May lose interest or delegate to someone else while pursuing a newer, more attractive project.

WHAT DOES ALL THIS MEAN?

The purpose of your Path Elements Profile™ is not to put you in a box or place a label on you that limits your potential. Neither is it meant to excuse or justify. The goal is to help you understand your naturally motivated behaviors and your best environment and situation for success in relationship to others. Sometimes, we unfairly judge people's motives because we don't clearly understand their behaviors. As a result of knowing yourself better, you will also understand others' needs and wants and motivations.

When we understand ourselves and others—our friends, family, neighbors, and coworkers—we are more capable of doing our best and avoiding stressful situations in our lives. We can also learn to rely on the strengths of others and welcome their helpful influence in our lives.

Before you go further, *stop* and return to the first page of your report. Scan through the pages and—using a pen, pencil, or highlighter—circle the *strengths* that you believe accurately describe you. Refer primarily to your general description and your essential element(s). Not all of them will apply, but you'll begin to recognize yourself as you read. Additionally, when you read a *challenge* that you recognize applies to you, check it as something you are going to work on for better balance in your life.

Continue reading and marking until you reach this spot again. Then, move on to the next two pages, where you will finally create an Action Plan based on your Path Elements Profile™.

My Personal Growth and Improvement Plan

Identifying Your Strengths

1. Review the strengths you circled and select four that best describe your talents. List them below as bullets or short phrases.

Wind (Essential Element)

-
-
-
-

Fire (Supporting Essential Element)

-
-
-
-

2. When you are able to operate from these strengths, what positive outcomes occur?

3. In what areas do you need to use these strengths now?

4. What strengths do you sometimes rely on too heavily, and what challenges or problems surface when this occurs?

Identifying Your Challenges

    1. List four of your challenges that you checked in your report.

Wind (Essential Element)

-
-
-
-

Fire (Supporting Essential Element)

-
-
-
-

       How are these behaviors or natural tendencies affected by stress?

    2. How do you want others to respond to you when you are demonstrating these behaviors?

    3. What are some actions you can take to be more effective in your areas of challenge?

    4. What are some actions you can take to work around some of your areas of challenge?

Understand and Value Others
by
Recognizing the Contributions of Each Element

Life could not exist if we lacked even one of these four elements on our planet. We need all of them—**Earth, Water, Wind,** and **Fire.**

Likewise, we need characteristics from all four elements in our lives to be successful. In some cases we will need to adapt for short periods to use behaviors from some of our non-natural elements. In other situations, we need to surround ourselves with people who have different elemental profiles and therefore strengths that are different from ours.

As you have learned already and as shown below, the traits of each element are different. Equally important, the contributions of each element are essential for group and team success. Look at the chart below and recognize the benefits your profile provides—and also appreciate how valuable the other elements are in complementing your talents.

Laurie Beth, I encourage you to rejoice in your own unique Wind/Fire characteristics. Develop your strengths to the fullest. Likewise, understand the impact your challenge areas may have on others with different elements. Celebrate the differences you see in others. Honor their strengths and give them room to be unique also. I wish you many blessings as you find, and follow, the Path4U in life.

APPENDIX III

SAMPLE PEP CHARTS

Following are sample charts for each of the Elemental Combinations.

EarthEarth, shown below are your scores for the four elements

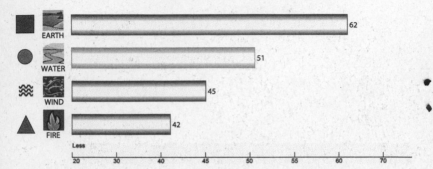

EarthEarth, by comparing the bar graphs above you can see that your strongest Element is EARTH. Like the EARTH, you prefer a grounding point that is steady and solid. You are predictable, stable, and slow to change. You store and save, and you work to protect your resources. In your environment, you tend to prefer things that are basic, trustworthy, constant, proven, and validated. Order and detail are important to you.

EARTH tends to focus its energies on completing tasks and sets very high measurements for the quality of its own work. Expects perfection from itself and imposes that standard on others, as well. Strives for more efficiency by creating processes and systems and wants facts instead of guesses or opinions. Listens carefully for data and statistics.

Typically, EARTH is modest, precise, observant, accurate, logical, conscientious, and consistent. Tends to avoid drawing attention, takes a realistic view, and is more serious and reflective in its thoughts. This Element values accuracy and wants to be prepared in advance, preferring to operate on a schedule instead of flexibly. Its approach to making decisions is systematic, rather than instinctive.

In the next four pages, you will learn more about your nature and also the characteristics of the other elements and how you can work with and relate best to each of them. You will also discover how to draw from each of the four elements to enrich your life. Let's begin with your most Essential Element.

EarthWater, shown below are your scores for the four elements

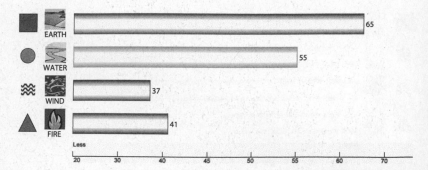

	EARTH	65
	WATER	55
	WIND	37
	FIRE	41

Less
20   30   40   45   50   55   60   70

EarthWater, by comparing the bar graphs below, you can see that your strongest Elements are EARTH and WATER. These are both slower-paced influences. Like the EARTH, you prefer a grounding point that is steady and solid. You are predictable, stable, and slow to change. You store and save, and you work to protect your resources. In your environment, you tend to prefer things that are basic, trustworthy, constant, proven, and validated. Order and detail are important to you. Like WATER, you tend to "go with the flow." As WATER can take on several forms in different environments, you adapt yourself to various situations. The image you present to others is calmness -- like a peaceful lake -- even though you may have great depth and activity beneath the surface. You are loyal, supportive, and move at your own pace.

EARTH-WATER draw from two Elements: EARTH carefully completes tasks with accuracy and high standards. WATER focuses on helping, encouraging, and supporting others. The combination of these traits means this Element likes processes, systems, and statistics -- but looks for balance and includes others' viewpoints, attitudes, and opinions to achieve consensus.

The EARTH element in EARTH-WATER is modest, logical, consistent, serious and reflective -- preferring to operate on a schedule instead of flexibly. WATER's fulfillment is derived from relationships, demonstrating loyalty and self-sacrifice in establishing friendships. The blended Element of EARTH-WATER responds to issues objectively while showing increased sensitivity to the needs and concerns of people.

In the next four pages, you will learn more about your nature and also the characteristics of the other elements and how you can work with and relate best to each of them. You will also discover how to draw from each of the four elements to enrich your life. Let's begin with your most Essential Element.

EarthWind, shown below are your scores for the four elements

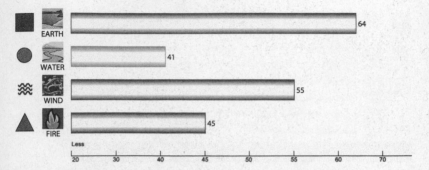

EarthWind, by comparing the bar graphs above you can see that your strongest Elements are EARTH and WIND which can present conflicting influences: EARTH is slow paced and task oriented, while WIND is fast-paced and people-oriented. Understanding how these 2 Elements oppose and support each other will help you make best use of this dynamic style.

Like the EARTH, you prefer a grounding point that is steady and solid. You store and save, and you work to protect your resources. Order and detail are important to you. But at times, like the WIND, you prefer moving quickly and having a visible impact. You are exciting, and may even be spontaneous, bringing energy to events and situations. Your passion about your beliefs will draw people to you, but may also cause you to ignore boundaries at times.

EARTH-WIND people draw from 2 Elements: EARTH prefers to complete tasks with high standards for itself and others, wants facts instead of guesses or opinions, and listens carefully for data and statistics. WIND focuses on what it experiences, moves at a fast pace, expresses ideas and makes decisions more emotionally than logically.

The EARTH element is analytical, cautious, efficient, and looks for ways to improve a process. Is quiet and unemotional, considerate of others yet objective, and guards its privacy. The WIND Element in EARTH-WIND is enthusiastic, persuasive, inspiring, creative, outspoken, idealistic, trusting, and open to new ideas. Understanding these opposing natures will help in maintaining priorities and focus.

In the next four pages, you will learn more about your nature and also the characteristics of the other elements and how you can work with and relate best to each of them. You will also discover how to draw from each of the four elements to enrich your life. Let's begin with your most Essential Element.

EarthFire, shown below are your scores for the four elements

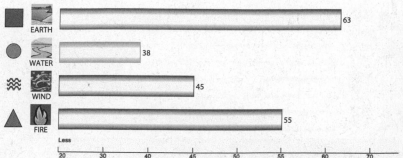

EarthFire, by comparing the bar graphs below, you can see that your strongest Elements are EARTH and FIRE. These are both task-oriented influences. Like the EARTH, you prefer a grounding point that is steady and solid. You are predictable, stable, and slow to change. You store and save, and you work to protect your resources. In your environment, you tend to prefer things that are basic, trustworthy, constant, proven, and validated. Order and detail are important to you. Like FIRE, you are capable of massive, sweeping action resulting in significant, widespread change. You are bold, direct, confident, and eager to be in charge of your destiny. To accomplish this, you seek choice and control of every situation, directing people and actions to obtain the desired result. Bottom-line results are important to you.

EARTH-FIRE draws from two elements: EARTH carefully completes tasks with accuracy and high standards. FIRE takes risks to overcome obstacles and achieve goals. The combination of these traits means this blended Element likes processes, systems, and statistics -- but can change methods to get results. Sees the big picture and the details that complete it.

The EARTH element in EARTH-FIRE is modest, logical, consistent, serious and reflective -- preferring to operate on a schedule instead of flexibly. Its FIRE element is pioneering, visionary, and competitive, confronting problems head-on and evaluating results, not intentions. Follows through on careful plans, achieving results based on challenge and reward.

In the next four pages, you will learn more about your nature and also the characteristics of the other elements and how you can work with and relate best to each of them. You will also discover how to draw from each of the four elements to enrich your life. Let's begin with your most Essential Element.

WaterEarth, shown below are your scores for the four elements

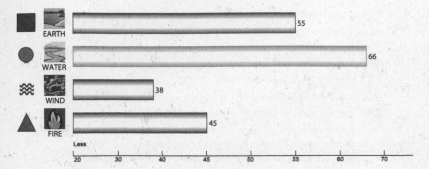

WaterEarth, by comparing the bar graphs below, you can see that your strongest Elements are WATER and EARTH, which are both slower-paced influences. Like WATER, you tend to "go with the flow." As WATER can take on several forms in different environments, you adapt yourself to various situations. The image you present to others is calmness -- like a peaceful lake -- even though you may have great depth and activity beneath the surface. You are loyal, supportive, and move at your own pace. Like the EARTH, you prefer a grounding point that is steady and solid. You are predictable, stable, and slow to change. You store and save, and you work to protect your resources. In your environment, you tend to prefer things that are basic, trustworthy, constant, proven, and validated. Order and detail are important to you.

WATER-EARTH draws from two Elements: WATER focuses on supporting, and fulfillment is derived from relationships. This Element demonstrates self-sacrifice in establishing friendships. EARTH prefers to complete tasks with high standards for itself and others, wants facts instead of guesses or opinions, and listens carefully for data and statistics.

The WATER Element in WATER-EARTH is a team player and good listener, avoids conflict and takes a practical approach to solving problems. The EARTH element is analytical, cautious, efficient, and looks for ways to improve a process. Is quiet and unemotional, considerate of others yet objective, and guards its privacy.

In the next four pages, you will learn more about your nature and also the characteristics of the other elements and how you can work with and relate best to each of them. You will also discover how to draw from each of the four elements to enrich your life. Let's begin with your most Essential Element.

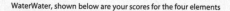

WaterWater, shown below are your scores for the four elements

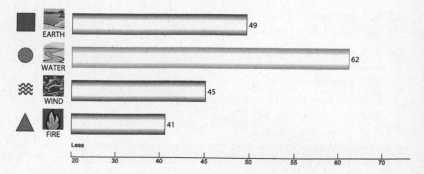

WaterWater, by comparing the bar graphs below, you can see that your strongest Element is WATER, which is people-oriented and slower-paced. Like WATER, you tend to "go with the flow." As WATER can take on several forms in different environments, you adapt yourself to various situations. The image you present to others is calmness -- like a peaceful lake -- even though you may have great depth and activity beneath the surface. You are loyal, supportive, and move at your own pace.

WATER people tend to focus their energies on helping, encouraging and supporting others. Their sense of fulfillment is derived from their relationships, and they demonstrate loyalty and self-sacrifice in establishing friendships. Balance is important to them, and they include others' viewpoints, attitudes, and opinions to arrive at a consensus. This Element puts out fires and cools things down when situations become heated.

Typically, WATER prefers to be a team player, avoids conflict and takes a practical approach to solving problems. Tends to be a good problem solver because it listens and wants to help. Often, this Element remains patient when others become frustrated and short-tempered. Its approach to solving problems is practical, wanting to complete a project before taking on another one.

In the next four pages, you will learn more about your nature and also the characteristics of the other elements and how you can work with and relate best to each of them. You will also discover how to draw from each of the four elements to enrich your life. Let's begin with your most Essential Element.

WaterWind, shown below are your scores for the four elements

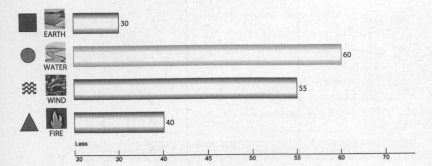

WaterWind, by comparing the bar graphs below, you can see that your strongest Elements are WATER and WIND, which are both people-oriented influences. Like WATER, you tend to "go with the flow." As WATER can take on several forms in different environments, you adapt yourself to various situations. The image you present to others is calmness -- like a peaceful lake -- even though you may have great depth and activity beneath the surface. You are loyal, supportive, and move at your own pace. Like the WIND, you prefer moving quickly and having a visible impact. You are exciting, spontaneous, and bring energy to events and situations. You tend to ignore boundaries, and people get swept up in your ideas. In your environment, you prefer fast action and immediate results.

WATER-WIND draws from two Elements: WATER focuses on supporting others and fulfillment is derived from relationships. This Element demonstrates self-sacrifice in establishing and maintaining friendships. WIND prefers to move at a fast pace, making decisions and expressing ideas more emotionally than logically. The combination of these traits usually results in a people person who is accepting, optimistic, and energetic.

The WATER Element in WATER-WIND is a team player and good listener, avoids conflict and takes a practical approach to solving problems. Its WIND Element is enthusiastic, persuasive, creative, idealistic, trusting, and open to new ideas. The blended Element of WATER-WIND is usually encouraging and inspiring, practical yet imaginative, and uses care and humor to encourage involvement and participation.

In the next four pages, you will learn more about your nature and also the characteristics of the other elements and how you can work with and relate best to each of them. You will also discover how to draw from each of the four elements to enrich your life. Let's begin with your most Essential Element.

WaterFire, shown below are your scores for the four elements

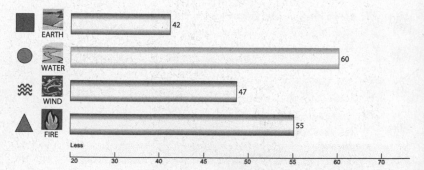

WaterFire, by comparing the bar graphs above you can see that your strongest Elements are WATER and FIRE, which can present conflicting influences: WATER is slower-paced and people-oriented, while FIRE is faster-paced and task-oriented. Understanding how these two Elements oppose and support each other will help you make best use of this dynamic style. Like WATER, you tend to "go with the flow.". As WATER can take on several forms in different environments, you adapt yourself to various situations. The image you present to others is calmness -- like a peaceful lake -- even though you may have great depth and activity beneath the surface. You are loyal, supportive, and move at your own pace. Like FIRE, you are capable of massive, sweeping action, resulting in significant, widespread change. You are bold, direct, confident, and eager to be in charge of your destiny. To accomplish this, you seek choice and control of every situation, directing people and actions to obtain the desired result. Bottom-line results are important to you.

WATER-FIRE draws from two Elements: WATER focuses on supporting, and fulfillment is derived from relationships. This Element demonstrates self-sacrifice in establishing friendships. FIRE takes risks to overcome obstacles and achieve goals. The combination of these traits likes to serve and encourage but is willing to step in and lead where leadership is inadequate.

The WATER Element in WATER-FIRE is a team player and good listener, avoids conflict and takes a practical approach to solving problems. Its FIRE element is pioneering, visionary, and competitive, confronting problems head-on and evaluating results, not intentions. The blend of these Elements results in a caring problem-solver who uses practical methods and a direct approach to get things done.

In the next four pages, you will learn more about your nature and also the characteristics of the other elements and how you can work with and relate best to each of them. You will also discover how to draw from each of the four elements to enrich your life. Let's begin with your most Essential Element.

WindEarth, shown below are your scores for the four elements

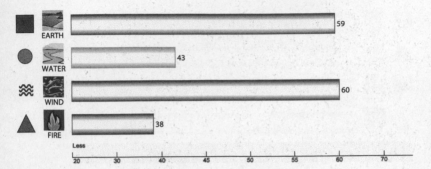

WindEarth, by comparing the bar graphs above you can see that your strongest Elements are WIND and EARTH, which can present conflicting influences: WIND is fast-paced and people-oriented, while EARTH is slower-paced and task-oriented. Understanding how these 2 Elements oppose and support each other will help you make best use of this dynamic style.

Like the WIND, you prefer moving quickly and having a visible impact. You are exciting, spontaneous, and bring energy to events and situations. Your passion about your beliefs will draw people to you, but may also cause you to ignore boundaries at times. Like EARTH , You store and save, and you work to protect your resources. In your environment, you tend to like things that are trustworthy and proven, but you also have a very strong desire to be creative.

WIND-EARTH people draw from two Elements: WIND focuses on what it experiences, moves at a fast pace, expresses ideas and makes decisions more emotionally than logically. EARTH prefers to complete tasks with high standards for itself and others, wants facts instead of guesses or opinions, and listens carefully for data and statistics.

The WIND Element in WIND-EARTH is enthusiastic, persuasive, inspiring, creative, outspoken, idealistic, trusting, and open to new ideas. The EARTH element is analytical, cautious, efficient, and looks for ways to improve a process. Is quiet and unemotional, considerate of others yet objective, and guards its privacy.

In the next four pages, you will learn more about your nature and also the characteristics of the other elements and how you can work with and relate best to each of them. You will also discover how to draw from each of the four elements to enrich your life. Let's begin with your most Essential Element.

WindWater, shown below are your scores for the four elements

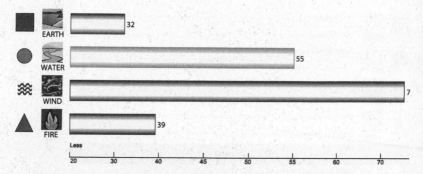

EARTH 32

WATER 55

WIND 7

FIRE 39

Less

20 30 40 45 50 55 60 70

WindWater, by comparing the bar graphs below, you can see that your strongest Elements are WIND and WATER, which are both people-oriented influences. Like the WIND, you prefer moving quickly and having a visible impact. You are exciting, spontaneous, and bring energy to events and situations. You tend to ignore boundaries, and people get swept up in your ideas. In your environment, you prefer fast action and immediate results. Like WATER, you tend to "go with the flow." As WATER can take on several forms in different environments, you are able to adapt yourself to various situations. The image you present to others is calmness -- like a peaceful lake -- even though you may have great depth and activity beneath the surface. You are loyal, supportive, and move at your own pace.

WIND-WATER draws from two Elements: WIND focuses on what it can see and feel, moving forward at a fast pace. Is friendly, talkative, outgoing, and optimistic. WATER demonstrates self-sacrifice in establishing friendships and supporting relationships. The combined Element is very people-oriented - both enthusiastic and sensitive to feelings of others.

The WIND Element in WIND-WATER is enthusiastic, persuasive, inspiring, creative, outspoken, idealistic, trusting, and open to new ideas. Its WATER Element is a team player and good listener, avoids conflict and takes a practical approach to solving problems. The blended Element of WIND-WATER is funny and warm and sympathetic and impulsive in dealing with people and their problems.

In the next four pages, you will learn more about your nature and also the characteristics of the other elements and how you can work with and relate best to each of them. You will also discover how to draw from each of the four elements to enrich your life. Let's begin with your most Essential Element.

WindWind, shown below are your scores for the four elements

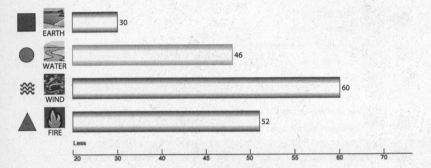

WindWind, by comparing the bar graphs below, you can see that your strongest Element is WIND, which is people-oriented and fast-paced. Like the WIND, you prefer moving quickly and having a visible impact. You are exciting, spontaneous, and bring energy to events and situations. You tend to ignore boundaries, and people get swept up in your ideas. In your environment, you prefer fast action and immediate results.

WIND people focus their energies on what they can see and feel and touch. This Element prefers to move forward and at a fast pace, measuring the quality of their work by its acceptance and effect on others. Is friendly, talkative, outgoing, optimistic, and works well with others. Operates from its heart rather than from its head, making decisions and expressing ideas more emotionally than logically.

Typically, WIND is enthusiastic, persuasive, inspiring, creative, outspoken, idealistic, trusting, and open to new ideas. Tends to draw attention because this Element can be fun, excitable, and involving. Admires verbal persuasiveness and ability to influence, and exercises these skills. Often make decisions based on endorsements by people it admires and are willing to try almost anything to see if it will succeed.

In the next four pages, you will learn more about your nature and also the characteristics of the other elements and how you can work with and relate best to each of them. You will also discover how to draw from each of the four elements to enrich your life. Let's begin with your most Essential Element.

WindFire, shown below are your scores for the four elements

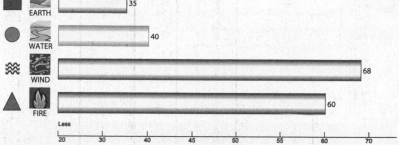

WindFire, by comparing the bar graphs below, you can see that your strongest Elements are WIND and FIRE, which are both fast-paced influences. Like the WIND, you prefer moving quickly and having a visible impact. You are exciting, spontaneous, and bring energy to events and situations. You tend to ignore boundaries, and people get swept up in your ideas. In your environment, you prefer fast action and immediate results. As FIRE, you are capable of massive, sweeping action resulting in significant, widespread change. You are bold, direct, confident, and eager to be in charge of your destiny. To accomplish this, you seek choice and control of every situation, directing people and actions to obtain the desired result. Bottom-line results are important to you.

WIND-FIRE draws from two Elements: WIND focuses on what it can see and feel, moving forward at a fast pace. This Element is friendly, talkative, outgoing, optimistic and works well with others. FIRE is motivated by overcoming obstacles and setting the pace to lofty goals. Takes risks, tends to see the big picture and delegates the details that complete it. The combined Element...

The WIND Element in WIND-FIRE is enthusiastic, persuasive, inspiring, creative, outspoken, idealistic, trusting, and open to new ideas. Its FIRE element is pioneering, visionary, and competitive, confronting problems head-on and evaluating results, not intentions. The blended Element of WIND-FIRE is a motivator, persuader and networker, coupling people skills with sharp focus.

In the next four pages, you will learn more about your nature and also the characteristics of the other elements and how you can work with and relate best to each of them. You will also discover how to draw from each of the four elements to enrich your life. Let's begin with your most Essential Element.

FireEarth, shown below are your scores for the four elements

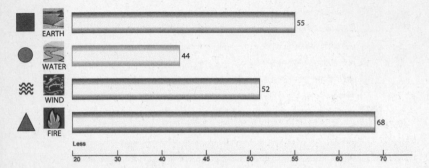

EARTH   55

WATER   44

WIND   52

FIRE   68

Less
20   30   40   45   50   55   60   70

FireEarth, by comparing the bar graphs below, you can see that your strongest Elements are FIRE and EARTH, which are both task-oriented influences. Like FIRE, you are capable of massive, sweeping action resulting in significant, widespread change. You are bold, direct, confident, and eager to be in charge of your destiny. To accomplish this, you seek choice and control of every situation, directing people and actions to obtain the desired result. Bottom-line results are important to you. Like the EARTH, you prefer a grounding point that is steady and solid. You are predictable, stable, and slow to change. You store and save, and you work to protect your resources. In your environment, you tend to prefer things that are basic, trustworthy, constant, proven, and validated. Order and detail are important to you.

FIRE-EARTH draws from two Elements: FIRE overcomes obstacles and achieves lofty goals, creating activity and setting the pace. This Element sees the big picture and delegates details. EARTH completes tasks with very high standards for self and others, striving for efficiency, creating processes and systems, and listening carefully for data and statistics.

The FIRE Element in FIRE-EARTH is pioneering, adventurous, visionary, intense, competitive, and outspoken, confronting problems head-on, and evaluating results, not intentions. The EARTH element is analytical, cautious, efficient, and looks for ways to improve a process. It is also quiet and unemotional, objective, and guards its privacy.

In the next four pages, you will learn more about your nature and also the characteristics of the other elements and how you can work with and relate best to each of them. You will also discover how to draw from each of the four elements to enrich your life. Let's begin with your most Essential Element.

FireWater, shown below are your scores for the four elements

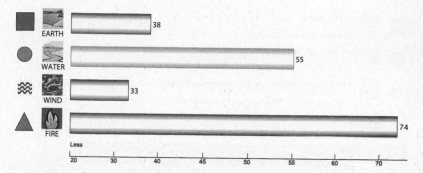

EARTH 38

WATER 55

WIND 33

FIRE 74

Less
20   30   40   45   50   55   60   70

FireWater, by comparing the bar graphs above you can see that your strongest Elements are FIRE and WATER which can present conflicting influences: FIRE is fast paced and results oriented, while WATER is slower-paced and people-oriented. Understanding how these two Elements oppose and support each other will help you make best use of this dynamic style. Like FIRE, you are bold, confident, and eager to be in charge of your destiny. To accomplish this, you seek choice and control, directing people and actions to obtain the desired result. Achievement of challenging goals is important to you. Like WATER, you tend to "go with the flow." As WATER can take on several forms in different environments, you adapt yourself to various situations. You are loyal, supportive, and move at your own pace.

FIRE-WATER draws from two Elements: FIRE moves ahead to overcome obstacles and achieve goals. WATER derives fulfillment from relationships and demonstrates self-sacrifice in establishing friendships, supporting other. The combination of these traits enjoys getting things done and is willing to lead or serve to achieve the goal.

The FIRE Element is pioneering, visionary, and competitive, willing to confront problems head-on. WATER moderates FIRE's strong personality with a preference to avoid confrontation and take a more practical, team oriented approach to situations. The blend of these Elements results in a caring problem-solver who uses practical methods and a direct approach to get things done.

In the next four pages, you will learn more about your nature and also the characteristics of the other elements and how you can work with and relate best to each of them. You will also discover how to draw from each of the four elements to enrich your life. Let's begin with your most Essential Element.

FireWind, shown below are your scores for the four elements

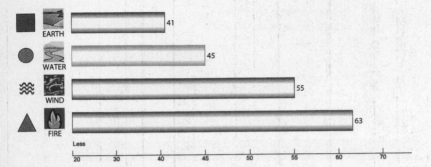

FireWind, by comparing the bar graphs below, you can see that your strongest Elements are FIRE and WIND, which are both fast-paced elements. Like FIRE, you are capable of massive, sweeping action resulting in significant, widespread change. You are bold, direct, confident, and eager to be in charge of your destiny. To accomplish this, you seek choice and control of every situation, directing people and actions to obtain the desired result. Bottom-line results are important to you. Like the WIND, you prefer moving quickly and having a visible impact. You are exciting, spontaneous, and bring energy to events and situations. People may be swept up into your ideas and in the excitement you may ignore boundaries. In your environment, you prefer fast action and immediate results.

FIRE-WIND draws from two Elements: FIRE overcomes obstacles and achieves lofty goals, creates activity and sets the pace. This Element sees the big picture and delegates details. WIND is enthusiastic, persuasive, inspiring, creative, outspoken, idealistic, trusting, and open to new ideas. Often makes decisions based on endorsements by admired people and will try almost anything to see if it will succeed.

The FIRE Element in FIRE-WIND is pioneering, adventurous, visionary, intense, competitive and outspoken, confronting problems head-on, and evaluating results, not intentions. The WIND Element is carefree, excitable, fun, involving, and tends to draw in other people. It is also a good networker - able to envision a project, then recruit and direct people who "want" to see it succeed.

In the next four pages, you will learn more about your nature and also the characteristics of the other elements and how you can work with and relate best to each of them. You will also discover how to draw from each of the four elements to enrich your life. Let's begin with your most Essential Element.

FireFire, shown below are your scores for the four elements

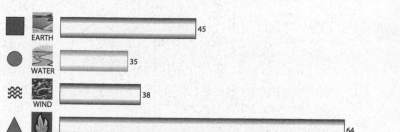

EARTH		45
WATER		35
WIND		38
FIRE		64

Less

20   30   40   45   50   55   60   70

FireFire, by comparing the bar graphs above, you can see that your strongest Element is FIRE, which is task-oriented and fast-paced. Like FIRE, you are capable of massive, sweeping action resulting in significant, widespread change. You are bold, direct, confident, and eager to be in charge of your destiny. To accomplish this, you seek choice and control of every situation, directing people and actions to obtain the desired result. Bottom-line results are important to you.

FIRE people are motivated by overcoming obstacles and achieving lofty goals -- they create activity and set the pace to reach them. They often are willing to take risks and may change methods and teams quickly if they do not get the results they expect. They tend to see the big picture and delegate the details that complete it. They are self-sufficient and determined to meet whatever challenges stand in their way.

Typically, FIRE people are pioneering, adventurous, focused, visionary, passionate, intense, competitive, and frankly outspoken. They tend to confront problems head-on, admire people who "walk the talk," and evaluate results, not intentions. They value commitment, meet deadlines, handle multiple projects at once, and want to determine their own agenda. They make decisions based on their perception of the challenge and reward.

In the next four pages, you will learn more about your nature and also the characteristics of the other elements and how you can work with and relate best to each of them. You will also discover how to draw from each of the four elements to enrich your life. Let's begin with your most Essential Element.

APPENDIX IV

A BRIEF HISTORY OF PERSONALITY THEORY

A Look at the Bible

Perhaps the first time the notion of differences in personality reared its head is in the biblical story of Cain and Abel, two genetically similar siblings who had very different personality likes and dislikes.

Jesus complemented the notion of different personalities when He told Simon, the fisherman, "You are Peter, and on this rock I will build my church." (Matt. 16:18) creating a prophetic word picture that has stayed with us for thousands of years. In the stories of Jesus, we are also introduced to James and John, who were called (for what one can only surmise to be due to observations of their temperaments) the "Sons of Thunder." Jesus also described Himself as "Living Water," a reference that I alluded to in my introduction.

The first official recorded use of personality testing dates back four-thousand years to the Mandarin dynasties of China, which used assessments to determine which members of the population would work well in government.

The Greek philosopher Plato (c 427–347) believed that having people take aptitude tests to determine which tasks they were best suited for would lead to the ideal state, as noted in his work titled *Republic*.

Hippocrates (460–377 B.C.), considered to be the founder of

Greek medicine, believed that illness could be attributed to the lovely notion of the percentage of bile in their system, and conceived of the four humors—blood, phlegm, yellow bile, and black bile.

The Greeks also believed that nature was made up of four elements—earth, air, water, and fire. These elements, as well as the four seasons, had corresponding humors. Four hundred years after the death of Hippocrates, a Roman doctor named Galen related Hippocrates's humoral theory to temperament. Hence were born the notions of sanguine (pleasant), phlegmatic (apathetic,), choleric (irritable), and melancholic (sad).

These theories had a major impact on Western medicine and psychology throughout the Middle Ages.

Development and interest in personality theories dwindled after the fall of the Roman Empire, as for the next one thousand years political, social, and religious constraints halted the freedom of thought and intellect.

During the Renaissance there were a revival of the Greek traditions and increased study in psychology and personality.

In the 1800s Granz Gall and Johann Spurzheim founded the pseudoscience of phrenology, relating bumps on the skull to personality. In the late 1800s, Francis Galton described methods for the measurement of character, including word associations and behavior-sampling techniques.

In the 1900s Sigmund Freud published *The Interpretation of Dreams* and laid a foundation of thought which is still influential today. In 1905 Carl Jung explored word-association tests to detect and analyze mental complexes.

During World Wars I and II, different assessments were developed to help select espionage agents and other field officers, and in the 1960s assessment tests were used to help select candidates for the Peace Corps.

The Rorschach's Inkblot Test (1921), and the Minnesota Multiphase Personality Inventory (MMPI) (1943) became major contributions to the understanding of personality types.

Abraham Maslow, the pioneer of the field of motivational psychology, developed the Social Personality Inventory and the Security-Insecurity Inventory in order to assess such factors as self esteem, dominance, and adaptablity. Maslow began to apply his psychological insights to industrial practices first on his brother's cooperage business in the 1940s.

In 1943 mother and daughter team Katherine Briggs and Isabel Myers developed the Myers Briggs Inventory, based largely on Carl Jung's work, claiming there are sixteen unique personality types in various combinations: Extraverted (E), Sensing (S), Thinking (T), Judging (J), or Introverted (I), Intuitive (IN), Feeling (F), and Perceiving (P).

During the 1960s personality assessments fell out of favor, due to charges of racial, economic, and gender bias which impacted scores. Nevertheless, the desire to understand differences in human personality continued, and continues to this day.

In 1985 John Holland developed the RIASEC model, maintaining that there are six types of vocational personalities and six work environments: Realistic (R), Investigative (I), Artistic (A), Social (S), Enterprising (E), and Conventional (C.)

Kathy Kolbe, daughter of the vocational testing pioneer, E. F. Wonderlic, has developed the Kolbe System, another highly influential assessment tool for problem solving and teams. Her emphasis is that problem-solving preferences are innate, and that strain and conflict arise when team members are not allowed to tackle problems in their preferred style.

Another popular psychological assessment is the DISC inventory, which assesses personality types based on Dominance, Influencing, Steadiness, and Conscientiousness.

Obviously, there are hosts of other assessments not included here. My goal was to give a brief overview of the field itself, showing the development in theories, and their roots.

Sources:

Edward Hoffman, Ph. D, *Psychological Testing at Work* (New York:

McGraw-Hill, 2002).

Lewis R. Aiken, *Human Differences* (Mahway, New Jersey: Lawrence Erlbaum Associates, Publisher, 1999).

ACKNOWLEDGMENTS

This book would not have come into being without the coordinated efforts of many incredible people. I first want to thank my agent and soul/friend, Terry Barber, whose continued faith in me and my ideas has given me euphoria in high winds and encouragement on the days when no wind seemed to be blowing. Thank you for using your cell phone on the Scottsdale golf course to torment Victor Oliver into taking a chance on this unorthodox idea. Thank you to Victor for overlooking Terry's taunts and being able to see for himself the value of using the elements to help people communicate and understand one another. Thank you to Jonathan Merkh for advancing the cause from day one at Thomas Nelson, and for always looking like he just stepped out of a *GQ* magazine ad as he hands me yet another contract to sign. Thank you to Kristen Lucas for being such a kind and gentle and knowing editor. Thank you to the awesome marketing and sales team at Thomas Nelson, including Scott Harris, Jennifer Willingham, and Jana Burson. Thank you to Belinda Bass and Pamela Clements for working with me on the cover design.

For the first time ever I had the privilege of engaging research workers to add weight and substance to my hunches and intuition.

I will always remember Jacque Salomy faithfully walking up the driveway in 110-degree heat, hand-delivering the first batch of her many wonderful gleanings. Thank you to ever patient and flexible Ellen Opitz, whose research and typing skills made my work so much easier. Thank you to Traci Price, who plowed through many books and articles, even when her grandmother was ill, in order to help me meet my deadline. Thank you to my niece, Tara Ivey, who, as always, came through in a pinch for me, assisting me with various fact checking and historic overviews of personality theory and testing.

I owe a special debt of gratitude to Jerry Mabe, Lee Ellis, and Sue Clark, who so patiently spent an entire summer last year helping bring me up to speed technologically with our online Path Elements Profile assessment. Thank you, Lee, for your vision of our working together, even when I was still wet behind the ears regarding the language and beauty of online assessments. Thank you, Jerry, for being willing to work so hard so we could all get farther faster, and for teaching me that there really is a place in Georgia called Smack A_ _ Gap. (I am not making this up.)

Shelly Buckner has been pivotal in my life, helping deepen and renew my vision for helping people find their Path, as well as being instrumental in bringing our Path4Schools program to life. I am continually amazed and humbled by her total commitment to helping children, especially, find their Path "so we won't have to help them figure it out when they're fifty," she says.

Ioanna Morfessis has been a guiding and challenging light. Thank you to lovely Joyce Haver, who quietly goes about parting seas and opening doors where no doors were opened before in her efforts to advance the cause. Fordham Tucker has proven to be a map maker of the highest order, reluctantly meeting me at Ioanna's insistence and subsequently harnessing thousands of hours of work on my behalf. He keeps using the word *covenant* as it relates to my walk with God, but I suspect the word applies to him as well.

Marty Blubaugh is my knight in shining armor, whose vision for bringing the Path to the disenfranchised both astounded and inspired me. His aim proved true, and thanks to his vision, we are now working with at-risk youths in three states.

Rosario Munoz, aka "ChaCha," is my voice and representative to so many who call requesting speaking engagements, products, or where to find a book translation in Chinese. She handles each person as the gem he or she is, and keeps me current on everything from bill paying to her latest golf scores.

Ken Blanchard continues to delight, amaze, and encourage me with his vision of having everyone Lead Like Jesus. Thanks, Ken, for making me one of your leading ladies on the wonderful simulcasts.

Thank you as always to Catherine C. Calhoun, who perhaps did more than anyone else to set me on my career path—teaching me that faith requires actions, and actions in line with your highest gifts always honor God.

To my sister, Kathy Ivey, congratulations on your budding and meteoric rise as an artist. To my brother, Joe Jones, thank you for being in the Fourth of July parade with your wife, Barbara, and your dog, and for always reminding me that life is rich when it is lived with family, pets, and friends.

To Ben Ivey, Tara, Bennie, and Wade, thank you for loving me all these years.

To my mother, Irene Jones, thank you for always affirming and encouraging me with statements like "You have a voracious mind." I am so blessed to have been born into your love and joyful playfulness.

ABOUT THE AUTHOR

Laurie Beth Jones has written several bestselling books, including *Jesus, CEO; Jesus, Life Coach; The Path; Jesus in Blue Jeans;* and *Teach Your Team to Fish*. Her books have been *Business Week* and *Wall Street Journal* best sellers and have been translated into twelve foreign languages, with worldwide sales of one million copies.

Using practical wisdom, bursts of humor, and reality-based thinking, Ms. Jones has become one of the world's leading consultants for businesses that want to take their work—and their workers—to unparalleled levels of performance, satisfaction, and success. She lives out her mission daily, which is to "recognize, promote, and inspire the divine connection in myself and others."

OTHER COACHING TOOLS

Would you like Laurie Beth Jones as your personal coach? For information on her availability to coach you or your team, call Rosario Muñoz at (915) 541-6033, or contact us at **www.lauriebethjones.com**. Laurie Beth is available for keynote speaking, teambuilding sessions, or retreats.

Path Training Seminars

If you desire to learn how to help others get clear on their mission in life, or even help yourself become more clear, experiencing a Path Seminar may be just the hands-on, face-to-face, experiential process, and gift you need. Log on to our website for dates, times, and locations.

Path for Teens Program

This 30-week curriculum is ideal for parents, youth leaders, counselors and teachers who work with young people. Now being launched in multiple states, in partnership with schools, YMCAs, and other nonprofits, we are seeking partners to help raise up the next generation. Log on to **www.path4u.com** to learn more.

Path for Kids CD Activity Book, Children's Songs cassette, Kids Color the Songs

This CD rom offers numerous exercises and programs to help kids learn more about their gifts, talents, and their ability to serve others. We also have a Children Songs and coloring book available for the little ones.

Jesus, Life Coach

There was a time when only athletes had coaches. Now, everyone from CEOs to at-risk youth are being "coached." The International Coaching Federation—which began with only a handful of people—now boasts membership of over 5,000, and currently more than 150,000 people call themselves "Life Coaches." The benefits of coaching have been well documented, but having the right coach is critical.

Jesus had only three years to train the twelve disciples, yet in that time he managed to turn this ragamuffin group into "lean, clean marketing machines." Divided into four critical sections—Focus, Balance, Productivity, and Fulfillment—*Jesus, Life Coach* presents a faith-based coaching program with Jesus as the model. Delving into the principles Jesus used to transform those around him, the book offers proven strategies and countless applications for modern-day coaches.

0-7852-6190-7
Hardcover

0-7852-8783-3
Trade Paper

Jesus, CEO

Jesus, CEO: Using Ancient Wisdom for Visionary Leadership is a practical, step-by-step guide to communicating with and motivating people. It is based on the self-mastery, action, and relationship skills that Jesus used to train and motivate his team. It can be applied to any business, service, or endeavor that depends on more than one person to accomplish a goal, and can be implemented by anyone who dares.

This book launched it all with a bold assertion that Jesus of Nazareth was and is the ultimate Chief Executive Officer. Hitting the *Business Week* Bestseller list immediately upon publication, it has since been translated into thirteen foreign languages, and has been featured in *Time* magazine, *Business Week, Industry Week,* and *USA Today,* as well as on CNN and the BBC. Short chapters and simple questions spawned study groups worldwide.

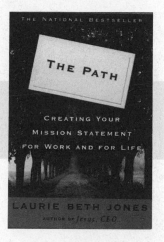

THE NATIONAL BESTSELLER

THE PATH

CREATING YOUR
MISSION STATEMENT
FOR WORK AND FOR LIFE

LAURIE BETH JONES
AUTHOR OF *Jesus, CEO*

The Path

In a world in which we are daily forced to make decisions that lead us either closer to or further from our goals, no tool is as valuable in providing direction as a mission statement—a brief, succinct, and focused statement of purpose that can be used to initiate, evaluate, and refine all of life's activities. A carefully thought out mission statement acts as both a harness and a sword—harnessing you to what is true about your life, and cutting away all that is false.

In *The Path*, Laurie Beth Jones provides inspiring and practical advice to lead readers through every step of both defining and fulfilling a mission. Jones offers clear, step-by-step guidance that can make writing a mission statement take a matter of hours rather than months or years.

The Path Training Seminars and Path for Teens Program are based on this book.

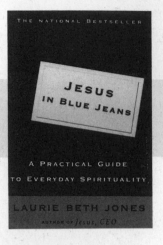

Jesus in Blue Jeans

Jesus in Blue Jeans is the conclusion to Laurie Beth Jones's trilogy, which began with her nationally bestselling books, *Jesus, CEO* and *The Path*. In this book, Laurie turns from the business world to everyday existence and reveals numerous ways of attaining spirituality and grace in our personal lives through the teachings of Jesus.

Following the example of Jesus—a "CEO" who took a disorganized "staff" of twelve and built a thriving enterprise—Laurie Beth Jones details a simple, profound, fresh, and often humorfilled approach to motivating and managing others.

Jesus Entrepreneur

One of the biggest workplace trends of the last few years has been the hunger for meaning and spirituality among people who once pursued their careers solely for money and prestige. Whether they work independently, for small businesses, or for major corporations, millions of Americans are now determined to use their talents to benefit the world as well as themselves. Consultant and bestselling author Laurie Beth Jones calls these people "spiritreneurs" because they fully bring their souls into their workplaces, usually with considerable initiative and risk. She also suggests that Jesus was the ultimate spiritreneur, because he gave up a comfortable living as a carpenter to pursue a new line of work that would really affect human lives.

With *Jesus Entrepreneur* Jones shows how we can all follow his example to pursue work that supports our deepest spiritual and personal beliefs. In addition to tales from the Bible, she also shares anecdotes from her own life, including real-world stories from the best and worst workplace situations she has encountered.

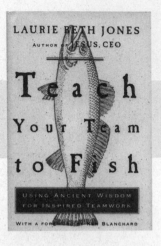

Teach Your Team To Fish

When Jesus called out to the fishermen, "Follow me, and I will make you fishers of men," He was about to transform each one of those recruits from someone who worked only for a daily paycheck to someone who was part of a larger team, working for eternity. As a teambuilder, you have been given perhaps the most challenging and rewarding work on earth today, which is teaching human beings to think and act like a team.

In *Teach Your Team To Fish* Laurie Beth Jones presents 47 clear principles designed to help you to excite, ground, transform and release your team, just as Jesus did.

My personal mission and vision is to create, nurture, and sustain Maximum Positive Impact in the Seven Pillars of Society, which are:

Business, Education, Healthcare, Faith and Service Organizations, the Government, the Mass Media, and the Disenfranchised.

My friends and associates and I will prayerfully do this by influencing though leaders in each of the Seven Pillars with this principle: Jesus of Nazareth is the ultimate role model for leadership and decision making in every aspect of life. Come join us in this work. Log onto our Website at www.lauriebethjones.com.

Blessings to you!
Laurie Beth Jones